# MEDITERRANEAN
# WINTER

# MEDITERRANEAN WINTER

THE PLEASURES OF

HISTORY AND LANDSCAPE

IN TUNISIA, SICILY, DALMATIA,

AND GREECE

Robert D. Kaplan

RANDOM HOUSE • NEW YORK

Library of Congress Cataloging-in-Publication Data

Kaplan, Robert D.
Mediterranean winter : the pleasures of history and landscape in
Tunisia, Sicily, Dalmatia, and Greece / Robert D. Kaplan.
p.    cm.
Includes index.
ISBN 0-375-50804-X
1. Mediterranean Region—Description and travel. 2. Classical
antiquities. 3. Civilization, Classical. 4. Mediterranean Region—
Antiquities.  I. Title.
D973.K37 2004      938—dc21      2003046691

Printed in the United States of America on acid-free paper
Random House website address: www.atrandom.com

2   4   6   8   9   7   5   3   1

First Edition

Book design by Meryl Sussman Levavi/Digitext

To William Whitworth and

Cullen Murphy

. . . *we came by the friendly light of a full moon to the little inn which we had left that morning before daybreak. Then, while the servants were busy preparing our supper, I spent my time in a secluded part of the house, hurriedly and extemporaneously writing all this down, fearing that if I were to put off the task, my mood would change on leaving the place, and I would lose interest in writing to you.*

— PETRARCH, "The Ascent of Mount
Ventoux," 26 April 1336

# PREFACE AND ACKNOWLEDGMENTS

This book is about a trip I took through Tunisia and Sicily in the winter of 1975–76, and other off-season trips to Dalmatia and parts of Greece as early as 1971 and as late as 1978. Limited sections of the narrative borrow also from trips in the 1980s and 1990s. My traveling companions were not always the same; nor were the circumstances. The overwhelming majority of these journeys were taken in my late teens and early twenties. I have fused them into a single narrative for the sake of readability.

Small portions of this manuscript have been adapted from two articles I wrote for *The New York Times:* "Chapels Recall Byzantine Era in Athens," October 26, 1980; and "Dubrovnik, a Glorious Phoenix," September 13, 1998.

I thank my agent, Carl D. Brandt, and my editor at Random House, Joy de Menil, for their wise advice and support. Cullen Murphy, managing editor of *The Atlantic Monthly*, provided additional editorial guidance. Thanks are also due to Ann Godoff, Kate Medina, and the staff at Vintage paperbacks—Luann Walther, Martin Asher, Andrew Miller, and David Hyde—who have been with me through many books. Victor Davis Hanson, an eminent classicist and military historian, and Aristide D. Caratzas, a scholar of the Byzantine and medieval eras, were kind enough to check the historical parts of the manuscript. Help also came from Corby Kummer, the Moye family, Annie Raskin, and my assistant, Elizabeth Lockyer. I am truly grateful to my wife, Maria Cabral, for putting up with my long absences over the years.

# CONTENTS

XIII

CONTENTS

6.

THE SPEECHLESS TEMPLE 95

7.

A CITY IN TERRA-COTTA 108

8.

SICILIAN JOURNEY 121

9.

HADRIAN'S VILLA 146

10.

DIOCLETIAN'S PALACE 152

11.

DUBROVNIK RISING 167

12.

MAGIC BOXES OF CRACKLING
CANDLELIGHT 179

13.

LITERARY BYZANTIUM 185

14.

THE MOREA AND NEOPLATONISM 201

15.

THE LAST PASHA OF THE
MEDITERRANEAN 223

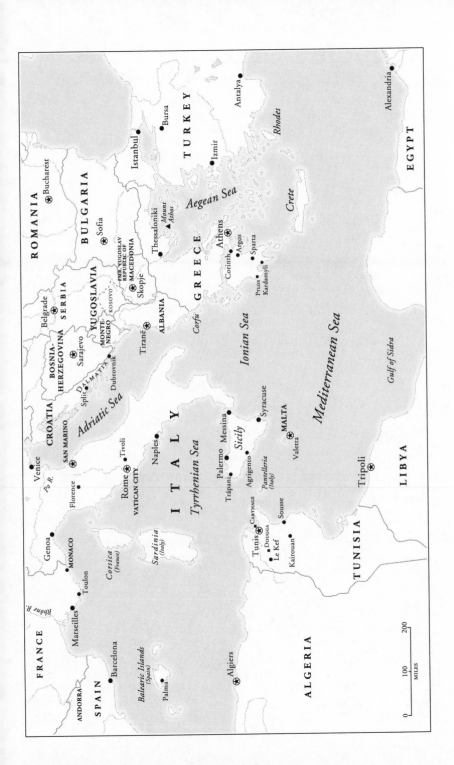

# MEDITERRANEAN
# WINTER

## THE TIGRESS

Divinity exists in beautiful memories: leaves like weight-less bronze, engraved with the year, falling amid the trees of Rodin's sculpture garden in Paris. For Rodin, the human body was the ultimate expression of nature, and nudity the opposite of decadence because it bore the glory and pain of the universe. Inside the artist's mansion, I recall torsos that, as Rainer Maria Rilke writes, were complete even though they lacked arms, and a haggard woman with a sag-ging belly and crumpled breasts who was beautiful. Rodin knew that limbs and youth are superfluous to beauty.

Rodin's "Old Woman" is the true goddess of travel. Her body is the tortured ruin of a lifetime, whose memories are intimated by her downward gaze. Her knowledge and experi-ence now have no material purpose except reflection. Indeed, the sculpture may represent a courtesan brooding over her sins: travel is where we truly meet ourselves. We remember what we must in order to endure, says the philosopher Henri Bergson. That is why so much of commonplace existence is forgotten, while our journeys never are.

∾

"The masses do not see the Sirens," Nikos Kazantzakis observes. "They do not hear songs in the air. Blind, deaf, stooping, they pull at their oars in the hold of the earth. But the more select, the captains, harken to a Siren within them . . . and royally squander their lives with her."

Kazantzakis' siren is a "merciless voice—the TIGRESS." She is his companion on all his journeys. She "digs her claws into my brain, and we reflect on all we have seen and all we have yet to see." Robert Graves calls her the "White Goddess," who can appear as a "she-wolf, tigress, mermaid or loathsome hag." The test of any writer's vision, Graves says, is "the accuracy of his portrayal" of her.

The goddess's physical beauty lies only in her eyes. Her allure is the life of the mind. For it is the yearning after comparisons and metaphors for each new object and landscape that sanctifies consciousness.

∾

Leaves falling on statues were my last memory of autumn for fourteen years. That evening I boarded a train south to Marseilles and instantly consigned Rodin's garden to the past. Like all diarists, I wrote down what I felt before moving on, while the mood of the place still dominated my thoughts.

Now I travel in retrospect: excavating only the most useful fragments. Thus, I will keep personal matters to a minimum.

I had recently graduated from college and was working at a small newspaper in Vermont. In the summer of 1975, I watched the civil war in Lebanon on the nightly news. In the hope of becoming a foreign correspondent, I applied for a job at the wire services, the television networks, and over a dozen large metropolitan newspapers. With little experience as a journalist and a degree from a middle-of-the-pack college, my résumé was forgettable. No one hired me.

I was restless. My father, a truck driver, had spent his twenties riding railway cars around the United States, earning a living as a horse-racing tout in forty-three of the lower forty-eight states. After a "big score" he would check into a first-class hotel, a big cigar in hand: twenty-four hours later he would be living a hobo's existence like so many others in the 1930s. He filled me with stories of his escapades in Depression-era America, and of the conquering image of a still-pastoral and naive nation, where the scams he ran were relatively innocent and people bought you a meal when you were down and out.

My father's last memory of travel was in 1942. He had just completed basic training in Fort Polk, Louisiana, and was heading north on a troop train for dispatch to Europe. At a rail junction near Cairo, Illinois, the sun was setting in rich colors over the prairie. Other trains were then converging from several tracks onto a single line that would take the soldiers to points along the East Coast where ships awaited. Across a wide arc, all he saw were trains and more trains, with soldiers looking out through every window as each train curved toward the other against a flat and limitless landscape lit red by the sun.

I had a traveling companion. Though we shared an intimacy that gave the journey its own enchantment, on another plane we remained two solitary beings filling up the pages of our respective notebooks. What follows is a record of that second, silent plane of existence, where the pronoun *I* is more appropriate than *we*.

I wandered through landscapes as though down the corridors of a museum, groping toward a vocation that I had never found in college. Because I now know much more about these places than when I first saw them, my recollection cannot help but be both enhanced and distorted.

෧෨

Rilke writes that the Greek and Roman galleries in the Louvre "revealed to Rodin radiant visions of an antique world of southern skies, a sea, heavy stone monuments from immemorial civilizations." Rodin had not simply copied the Greek and Roman style. He was heir to two millennia of Christian culture. His statues owe their powerful effect to the turmoil and agitation arising from the guilt of original sin. Thus, they lack the idealized serenity common to classical sculpture. I remember them because of their link to the ancient ruins and medieval churches that I saw afterwards in Tunisia and Sicily: places that drew me because of the books I read.

For those who, in Kazantzakis' words, "squander their lives" with the Tigress, the great events of life come from the books, rather than the people, one comes across. Some books show us a new world, others vindicate our own experience. Books can lead you astray, they can ruin you, they can deliver you from the strictures of your environment. Because some are so important one remembers perfectly the circumstances in which one found them, and read them.

You don't find the books that change your life by accident; nor by design. One finds them the way a ragpicker finds something useful in the garbage, or the way a hunter accidentally encounters his prey. The enterprise demands vigilance, says the philosopher Walter Benjamin: it takes practice to lose one's way in a city in order to discover something important about it.

I had strayed into a bookshop in Hanover, New Hampshire, on an October day of intense sunlight and broken shadows, melancholy despite the electric colors of the leaves. On a back shelf I found Gustave Flaubert's *Salammbô* and Michel Zeraffa's *Tunisia;* on a table near the front of the shop was Livy's *The War with Hannibal.* Henceforth, I encountered civilizations and empires: Numidian, Roman, and Carthaginian; Vandal and Byzantine; Aghlabid, Zirid, and Hafsid. Also kings, generals, saints, false prophets, and wise men: Jugurtha, Scipio Africanus, Hannibal, Genseric, St. Augustine, Donatus, Justinian, Ibn Khaldun.

In *Salammbô,* Flaubert writes of a war between Carthage and its Libyan-led mercenaries, who rebelled in 241 B.C. His chilling descriptions of an organized state defending itself against an anarchic horde made a lasting impression on me. In Flaubert's hands, Tunisia became a land of monsters and ruins, blood and sensuality. He depicts mercenaries painted with vermilion "like coral statues"; soldiers snoring "open-mouthed" beside the burnt corpses of monkeys; lions crucified along a road; barbarians smearing butter and cinnamon on the faces of idols in celebration of a victory; and the sacrifice of children to appease the pagan god Baal. When the Carthaginian priestess Salammbô finds a Libyan mercenary leader alone in his tent, her body smells of "honey, pepper, incense, and roses," while the stench of nearby elephants wafts through a tear in the canvas. Flaubert's description of the effects of a thunderstorm upon a crowd, prior to the ritual slaughter of boys, provides a rare insight into the emotions behind child sacrifice.

The war that Livy records between Rome and Carthage occurred two decades after the one described by Flaubert. While many of the battles were fought in Sicily, the war climaxed in Tunisia. For millennia, Tunisia, with its command of the Sicilian Channel, guarded the whole of the western Mediterranean. That autumn I pored over maps of Tunisia and Sicily: two inviting fragments of land, with deserts, almond-clad mountains, and ruins. Their volatile inhabitants had embraced Christianity, the Donatist heresy, and Islam with equal passion. The two territories form the bottleneck of the Mediterranean, dividing it into east and west: each, as I would learn, with its own historical and cultural pattern.

I would fly to France and take a boat to Tunisia, with the aim of traveling about the Mediterranean. The winter stretched ahead of me like a lifetime. How to recapture the sense of endless possibilities before the accumulation of deeds to justify: when one was unaccountable to time because there was always time to make up for a mistake?

ᘒᘓ

On an icy midnight in November 1975 I boarded a train at the Gare de Lyon in Paris bound for Marseilles. At dawn, I awoke near Arles to the sting of salt air and olive trees against a soft sky the color of pressed grapes. Shaved rolling fields of the deepest vegetal green, immaculately sectioned by poplars, had dissolved into the confusion of sandy hillsides and sagging roofs of moldering clay. Northern Europe had vanished. I had $1,000 in traveler's checks and no return ticket.

I had left the newspaper in Vermont and would never hold another job. Like so many other free-lance journalists I would meet over the years, I was never to enjoy the social and professional status—or the generous travel budgets—of foreign correspondents for major media organizations. I read and studied on my own and sold articles to newspapers, which provided me just enough money to get by in youth hostels and cheap hotels, and to continue traveling. *Innovate* was the creed I was forced to adopt. Without money for transatlantic calls and before the era of fax machines and courier services, I relied on local post offices, where I found acceptance letters or rejection slips, checks or returned articles. My choices were driven by the contingencies of the moment. It was a life of radical freedom.

After the crowds and commotion of Marseilles' Saint Charles station, I tumbled straight into the city: down the station's steep marble staircase with its panoramic view of crowded thoroughfares that lead to the Old Port. Amid cheap department stores and plate-glass kiosks, where dark men in ski caps bought snacks labeled *halal*—"fit for Moslems"—I smelled garbage and the chilly breath of the Mediterranean for the first time. The wind blew under a leaden roof of clouds. I felt as cold as in Paris, and heard Arabic and French fired in staccato bursts like Italian. Trucks were unloading crates of fish and produce. I entered an unlit bar for a cup of coffee. Tables were stacked in the back. Broken, dusty mirrors were graced by art nouveau friezes. A pinball machine stood in the corner, where men gossiped and filled out lotto tickets. I found a hotel for the equivalent of four dollars: a faded yellow room with damp floors and exposed pipes. It stood on a narrow street of pizza joints where Arab men sold cheap watches and colognes in metal stalls.

Paris had been a clutter of gilded mirrors and perfectly arranged shops, a dense quilt of museums and cobblestones on certain streets. Marseilles felt like a raw wind, stripping away formalities and traditions, the vacuum filled by hustling, working-class Arab immigrants. Marseilles' rough edge was its seduction. It "perspires in the sun like a beautiful girl who does not take good care of herself," wrote Maupassant in the nineteenth century.

Marseilles was rogue waiters, plastic chairs, vinyl table cloths, and the smells of steaming mullet and eel. Life here was lived in the open: less attention was paid to interiors and their details. Greek sailors from Phocaea, on the coast of Asia Minor, had founded Marseilles in 600 B.C., attracted by its deep harbor protected on all sides by an amphitheater of hills. *Massalia* is Phoenician for "settlement," so perhaps the Phoenicians had arrived here first. Greek Massalia threatened Phoenician Carthage's zone of influence. Montesquieu writes of "great wars between Carthage and Marseilles over fishing grounds." The Greeks, though imperiled by surrounding Roman colonies in Gaul, nevertheless allied themselves with Rome against Carthage. Montesquieu goes on:

> The war the Romans waged against the Carthaginians in Spain was a source of wealth for Marseilles, which served as their storehouse. The ruin of Carthage and Corinth increased further the wealth of Marseilles; and, if it had not been for the civil wars in which one had blindly to choose a party, it would have been happy under the protection of the Romans, who were not jealous of its commerce.

Marseilles taught me that Mediterranean history was about power first, beauty second. The artistic monuments I had seen in the Louvre were the products of wealthy empires that mastered the hurly-burly of commerce and military strategy before they could produce great art. Except for what the French scholar Fernand Braudel calls "the leveling hegemony of Rome" (following its final defeat of Carthage in 146 B.C.), the Mediterranean throughout antiquity and the Middle Ages had been a stern document of balance-of-power politics. The poverty of its sandy soil had forced the peoples of the region to go abroad for conquest, yet neither the Carthaginians nor the Greeks, the Vandals, the Byzantines, the Venetians, or the Turks could control the entire sea. The city before me was a replica of that turbulent history: Arabs from North Africa, Italians, Spaniards, Greeks, Corsicans, and other immigrants had drifted to its unkempt streets, the human detritus of upheavals and trading ties, making Marseilles the most Mediterranean of cities.

In the spirit of ancient Phocaea, whose founding city Tacitus had described as equally crass, Marseilles was dedicated to mercantilism and had few public monuments. Those that there were reflected the needs of a population consumed with economic survival. The two nineteenth-century churches were heavy in style, their gloomy splendor exuding strength, not grace. Their interiors were jammed with ex-votos, for it was the promise of miracles that gave people the strength to face the next day. La Major (Sainte-Marie-Majeure) was a mock-Byzantine pile. It sat by the harbor near the site of a pagan temple dedicated to Diana. Nôtre Dame de la Garde was perched on an outcrop overlooking the city, its gilded statue of the Virgin visible from all points like a giant good luck charm.

La Canebière, the principal thoroughfare, was lined with cheap luggage and toy stores. Its name came from the Latin *cannabis,* an allusion to a rope-making factory that had existed nearby. I followed it to the Old Port, settled more than 2,500 years ago by Phocaean Greek sailors—a vast, rectangular sweep of oily-gray water bordered by peeling shuttered apartment buildings. I was pelted by rain and had no umbrella. One drop chased another so quickly that the sea water looked encrusted by rough glass. On the slippery esplanade, people in soggy work clothes queued for slabs of bass and mini-mountains of oysters under canvas awnings slapping loudly in the wind.

I felt the miserable cold of a night with little sleep and dreaded the thought of returning to a wet, unheated hotel room where my clothes wouldn't dry and where I had few others to change into. But soon after the rain halted, the sun broke through the clouds, and the harbor water calmed. The stench of fish and the sea momentarily overcame me, contracting the distance to other ports, reviving possibilities. My clothes began to dry as I walked toward the medieval barbicans that guarded the entrance to the outer sea.

An old lady with a kerchief was hanging clothes on a rooftop now that the rain had ceased. Old men with flat caps gathered in an alleyway to play *boules*. Amid such homespun normalities I felt vicariously part of the city. Seeing a city out of season is like finding a woman at home in her bathrobe without makeup: there is a feeling of both intimacy and letdown in which you may learn something vital. "Unlike halts in summer, winter sojourns bestow a kind of honorary citizenship," Patrick Leigh Fermor, a British authority on the Mediterranean, has written.

Now that the sun had reappeared, I felt that somehow I had come through my first crisis. I had not been robbed, had not lost my passport. I had merely suffered one of those fleeting bouts of loneliness, common to all travelers.

❧

I bought a second-class deck ticket for the twenty-five-hour voyage from Marseilles to Tunis. Hypnotic Middle Eastern music blared out of a raspy transistor as the ship began to sway, its slow, authoritative movement steering us up the ramp of the horizon. Men sat on bursting suitcases, barely kept together by blankets and rope. One was wearing pants with an alligator pattern, red socks, and a yellow sport jacket. Only after I had seen the elegant caftans and *chechias* worn by Tunisian men in their homeland did I realize that with little money or insight into European taste, these workers had simply bought what was affordable in the pseudo-western environment of Marseilles, or what had delighted them.

A wind splashed water onto the deck as we gained enough distance for Marseilles to emerge as it had not on land. I remember masses of rosy clay-tiled roofs, the busy harbor jostling with people, and the main dome and the four smaller ones of La Major, evincing the stalwart unity of a soldier holding a salute. Guarding the Old Port were two forts: St. Jean, built in the fourteenth century by the Knights of Jerusalem; and St. Nicolas, which went up in the seventeenth century on the order of Louis XIV. It was the universal pageant of human enterprise, the *to*ing-and-*fro*ing for profit backed up by religious faith and the sword.

Soon we were passing islands of naked limestone, dotted about with the staged precision of theater props, the tiniest among them the Île d'If, where Edmond Dantès, the hero of Alexandre Dumas' *The Count of Monte Cristo,* arrested on faked charges, had been held prisoner. We sailed on, the water turning from jade to darkest ink.

As Marseilles slipped away, both the wind and the tumult of conversation on deck died down. Even the transistor was turned off. People came up from the cabins and coalesced into small groups, pointed to this and that, until everyone eventually stopped talking as the last of the off-shore islands was reduced to a mote on the horizon. I thought of the gossiping that goes on before a funeral, and the sudden quiet as the service begins. The deck cleared after the sun had melted into a delta of lava flows.

Damp, salt air collected stickily on my face and the backs of my ears, and I was overcome by a queasy drowsiness. The floor of the ship repeatedly gave way under me, only to catch me as it rose once more. Soon people were vomiting in the ash trays stationed in the corridors, and stumbling everywhere. I tried to go on deck for fresh air but it had begun raining hard. Still, I remember looking out at the water, shivering in the rain for a minute or so. In its churning, black winter midst, even the storied Mediterranean seemed like a great ocean, remote from human history, as vast as space and echoing the sounds of chaos and eternity. One of the cliches about the Mediterranean is that it is "a sea within the measure of man." But that is not how it seemed to me that night, as I crossed a five-hundred-mile stretch of it.

I would learn later that the Mediterranean had been far from tamed by the Greeks and Romans, or the Spaniards, Venetians, and Ottomans, whose ships had plied its coastal areas only (and only in clement weather), with great stretches of the sea, in Braudel's phrase, remaining "as empty as the Sahara." In the late sixteenth century, it took two months to sail from Venice to the Holy Land. Formed by the collapse of coastal shelves, the Mediterranean has relatively few shallow areas, and a short distance from land plunges to oceanic depths: 14,450 feet off the coast of Greece. "Biologically exhausted," in the words of oceanographers, and without the coastal shelves to maintain large quantities of marine life, through much of history the Mediterranean supported few long-distance fishing fleets. That led to a shortage of good sailors and shipwrights, which, in turn, hampered exploration and made the sea more of a mystery.

Consequently, the Mediterranean became for humanity not a single sea but a series of smaller ones: the Adriatic, the Aegean, the Tyrrhenian, and so on, each with its own romantic allure. Often, the smaller and narrower the sea the greater its historical imprint, as humankind was able to master it and leave traces of its legacy. The Carthaginians, whose influence had encompassed this particular stretch of sea, had accomplished this feat only by plying the coast of North Africa westward all the way to Gibraltar, and then sailing eastward up the Spanish coast. The point at which I now looked out upon the water was barely known to the ancients, and thus was without myth or romance.

The Mediterranean climate is the result of two forces: the Sahara Desert and the Atlantic Ocean. The Sahara—only a few miles inland from the coast of North Africa—overwhelms the Mediterranean from the spring to the fall, accounting for the hot and dry air, glittering light, and immense blue skies that have drawn tourists and literary travelers for centuries. But from the fall till the spring it is the Atlantic influence that is predominant, with depressions slipping in from the west, stirred by the anticyclone over the Azores. I felt an Arctic loneliness as the rain crashed on my jacket. Down in the corridor, I curled up in a corner and fell asleep for a few hours until dawn.

The sun went slanting round the mighty year,
And freezing winter came, roughing the sea
With northern gales. . . .

When sometime afterwards I read those lines from Virgil's
*Aeneid,* I thought of my own brief experience at sea that night.
With this journey, I acquired the habit of searching for books
linked to the landscapes and seascapes through which I traveled. Reading became like surgery: a way of dissecting the surrounding landscape and my own motivations for being there.

Virgil writes, *Whatever comes, All Fortune can be mastered by
endurance.* Just as military officers who have known war firsthand can grasp more fully the meaning of Thucydides, only
after I married and had a family would I grasp what Virgil,
Homer, Tennyson, and others meant by the hardship of
travel. For the loneliness I had felt in Marseilles was merely
an intimation of what I would feel years afterwards, alone
and sick in a West African village on my son's birthday, or
stuck in Sudan during a coup with the borders closed and my
wife quite ill at home. Only with a home of my own could I
truly appreciate Virgil's description of Aeneas breaking loose
from the comfort and safety of Dido's palace in Carthage to
continue on his voyage; or Homer's description of Odysseus
preserving the memory of his house and family, despite the
allures of the road.

I woke to a calmer sea, what I took mistakenly for a sign
of a warmer climate, now that the ship was off the southern
coast of the Mediterranean. Sunlight pierced a hole through
the cloud dome onto the leaden expanse of water. Then for

hours we sailed up one of the great highways of history. From the little I had read at the time about Tunisia, I knew that through these waters had passed galleys from Phoenician Tyre, the triremes of Hannibal and his nemesis Scipio, the Byzantine fleet of Belisarius about to crush the Vandals in 534 A.D., Turkish pirates and others, testament to the fact that for much of human history the sea here had formed the strategic core of the western world. The ship entered the Gulf of Tunis, marked by Cape Farina, where Scipio had landed thirty thousand Roman troops in 204 B.C. in his quest to trap Hannibal. I spotted Bou Kornein, the "Two-horned Mountain," wrapped, as Flaubert had once imagined, in mysterious shadow. It was the legendary home of the Phoenician god Baal, a component of many Carthaginian names: Hanni*bal,* Hasdru*bal,* Iddi*bal* . . .

Colors infiltrated the water after the unpeopled grayness of the deeper depths. The funereal greens of firs and holm oaks gave the new landscape an air of restraint and profundity. The red soil was the color of spices. White villas completed a storybook setting, in which landmarks were easily recognizable and distances did not seem overwhelming.

Once again, the passengers gathered in silence on the deck. The water turned suddenly a muddy brown as the ship entered the port of La Goulette, which with its silos and oil tanks was like any port anywhere. The Moorish arches of the beige port building, a lone minaret, and the traditional red caps—*chechias*—worn by a few of the dock workers were the only indications that we were now in North Africa. The ship wheeled to its side, passing through the wind, as if the last barrier between us and the land. After the Romans had con-

quered Carthage, they gave their new colony the name
Africa, the Latinized version of the local Berber word *Ifriqa*.
For centuries, "Africa" meant the area of present-day Tunisia
before it did anything else.

Soon we were off the ship and the Tigress began to dig
her claws into my brain.

# 2

## THE WHITE FATHERS' MUSEUM

Proust writes that place-names help crystallize one's thoughts about "certain points on the earth's surface . . ." The name Parma evoked something "compact and glossy, violet-tinted, soft," while Florence meant "vernal scents" and "the genius of Giotto." For Diodorus, the Greek historian from Sicily, "Tunis" conjured up a white city on a chalky hill. I saw Tunis as the glow of gypsum lamps, shimmering and lime-washed mosques: a vaguely hostile mystery owing to the proximity of Muammar Qaddafi's Libya. The more elaborate and defining essences I would know only firsthand.

The lake that separated Tunis from the port of La Goulette, spanned by a causeway lined with pink flamingos, smelled of salt and mud. Next came the more delicate odors of anise, mint, and roasted chestnuts as my battered taxi slipped into a gridwork of belle epoque and art deco buildings, their grubby white facades like crumbling wedding cake. It was early evening and drizzling. I recall yellow headlights reflecting in puddles. There were flower sellers under fig trees, whispering their sales pitches in Arabic and French above the scream of cicadas. The city had the dreamy aura of suspended animation, a sleepy, mid-century French provincial town with trams creaking along narrow streets. A small crowd had gathered by the white plaster nudes of the National Theater to buy tickets for *La Bohème*. Some of the men and women resembled mannequins with petite waists and dripping features. Just about every Mediterranean civilization had invaded Tunisia, and pirates had brought captives from all over the seaboard to local harems, so the bloodlines were rich. Looking at people's faces, my head reeled from the history they contained.

The word "history" derives from the Greek *istoreo,* "to inquire." *Istoreo,* in turn, is related to the perfect tense form of the verb *oida,* which in archaic Greek meant "see," and later "know." Its cognate is the Latin word *video,* "see." Hence the primary meaning of "history" is: "that which I have seen and then known." The word "idea" also comes from this root. History that winter was something I saw before encountering it in books.

In 1975, Tunisian men wore ruby red *chechias* and flowing white robes, or *jibbahs.* A few even had a white jasmine tucked behind their ear, like a cigarette: a pagan custom from ancient Carthage that had survived Islam. It had a poetic and sexual effect without being perverse.

I saw only a few beggars. The city was not intimidating

or bursting at the seams like Marseilles. Tradition wrapped Tunis in a protective embrace. "Nowhere in Barbary," wrote a Frenchman in 1840, "do the Moors show so much tolerance and politeness." It was still so: something I would appreciate only years later after visiting Algeria.

My first meal in Tunisia was not couscous, but something more ubiquitous and essential to the Mediterranean landscape, a *casse-croûte:* a French loaf stuffed with oily tuna, parsley and anise, capers, fiery *harissa,* and black olives. The olive came to the Mediterranean from Mesopotamia and Persia. Mago, a Carthaginian agriculturalist often quoted by the Romans, directed that olive trees should be planted seventy-five feet apart, a testament to the fertility of the soil, given that most ancient olive trees were spaced only twenty feet apart. Never would I see as many olive trees and eat as many olives as in Tunisia. The same with dates, blood oranges, and red peppers.

The Tunis *medina* was integrated into the life of the capital like that of no other walled city in the Middle East. In its narrow streets one could find the finest restaurants but also the prime minister's office. After I became better acquainted with Greece, I would think of Tunis' old city as a Greek souk: its white stucco spareness, its doorways and window grilles painted sky-blue, with smells of jasmine, baked bread, and fragrant oil. Piles of esparto grass baskets and blue wire bird cages created a feeling of space in the narrowest alley. Missing was the abundance of heavy, intricately etched brassware and magenta colors of other oriental bazaars, with their burden of Near Eastern and Central Asian carpets. Here, the breath of Andalusia was stronger than that of Persia and Mesopotamia. This was all before the onslaught of "globalization" in the 1990s, when the local merchandise became nearly indistinguishable from that sold in Cairo or Jerusalem.

The shops offered spectacular views of the *medina* from their roofs. I walked onto a balcony of glassy tiles and twirling pomegranate-red columns inlaid with marble, sparkling from a recent rain. A cityscape of shallow white domes and minarets appeared to float below. The *medina* was a legacy of Hafsid Tunis.

One Berber horde after another had swept across north-west Africa, establishing a tenuous grip before giving way to the next. All had begun as militant religious sects fired by a passion for a stricter interpretation of Islam, and in the process of imposing their beliefs upon the nomads they became empires. In 1159, the fanatical Almohads—the name means "unitarians" or "absolute monotheists"—set out eastward from the Atlas Mountains in Morocco to conquer Ifriqiyah, as medieval Arab Tunisia was known. Ten thousand warriors entered Tunis. But in 1229, the Almohad dynasty began to disintegrate when a certain Zakariya, the local governor of Ifriqiyah, proclaimed his independence. Zakariya named his new emirate after his father, Abu Hafs. Under Zakariya's successors, the Hafsids conquered all of Almohad territory as far west as Fez in Morocco.

The Hafsid Empire was simply too big to remain united. By the end of the thirteenth century, it too began to disintegrate. New dynasties emerged that were to give Morocco, Algeria, and Tunisia their current dimensions. Still, the Hafsids were able to hold on in Tunisia until 1534, when Tunis fell to the corsair Khareddin ("Barbarossa"), an ethnic Greek from the island of Lesbos who had converted to Islam. The long rule of the Hafsids provided Tunisia with a modern identity to reinforce the legacies of Carthage and Rome. The Hafsids encouraged immigrants from Moorish Spain, who built the monuments and refurbished the coastal plain with fruit orchards. The city that Cervantes knew in the late sixteenth century that inspired him to write *Don Quixote*—about the time that Sinan Pasha officially claimed Tunis for the Ottoman Turks—was an urban jewel of 200,000 souls.

The more beautiful the landscape the more you want to devour its past and culture: all intellectual life rests ultimately on aesthetics. That was even more so in the case of Tunisia because its beauty had yet to be popularly transcribed. Unlike Italy or Greece, it never had a D. H. Lawrence or a Lawrence Durrell, while Norman Douglas wrote mainly about the desert oases.

☙❧

Soon after I arrived, I met a young man in a carpet shop who took me to his uncle's cafe, where he taught me *chkobbaa,* a game like cassino played with a forty-card deck. The cafe was next to Zitouna, the "Great Olive Tree Mosque," built in the ninth century by the Aghlabites, a dynasty that had originated in Iraq and brought its austere architecture with it. Bored with cards, I wandered into the mosque's central prayer hall, built with Corinthian columns retrieved from the ruins of Roman Carthage, their bases now cloaked with esparto grass mats. Pigeons dove from the walls as rain clouds gathered overhead. I remember admiring the monumental Arabic script from Kufah in Iraq, carved into the stone, as two small boys attempted to sell me several leather-bound religious commentaries.

The Olive Tree Mosque had housed a library of 36,000 volumes at a time when scholars and poets were drawn to the splendors of the Hafsid court. Following my visit to the mosque I came across the name Ibn Khaldun for the first time. He had often prayed in the Olive Tree Mosque and had strolled these very alleys as a youth, and again after he returned to Tunis from Fez and Granada as a middle-aged man.

Ibn Khaldun, born in 1332, was a writer, thinker, traveler, and historian of the caliber of the Italian Renaissance, though he lived in North Africa. He advised sultans and prime ministers not only in Ifriqiyah but also at the courts of Moorish Spain and the Maghreb, as Morocco was then known. His hardships and personal misfortunes were inextricable from his adventures. After mastering the Koran, studying its commentaries, and familiarizing himself with Arabic literature, he obtained employment at the Hafsid court in Tunis and at the age of twenty-three became a secretary to Sultan Abu Inan in Fez. There the sultan began to suspect his loyalty and threw him into prison, where he languished for two years until the sultan died. He then became a favorite of the new sultan, Abu Salem, but fell out of favor with the prime minister. That forced Ibn Khaldun to emigrate to Spain, where at Granada he was well treated by the ruler Ibn al Ahmar, whom Ibn Khaldun had once helped in Fez. Yet, the favors he received from Ibn al Ahmar excited the jealousies of the vizier, and Ibn Khaldun fled back to Africa. For the next decade he moved from place to place, was robbed by nomads, and finally took refuge with a tribe in present-day Algeria, giving him the solitude to write his masterpiece, the *Muqaddimah,* "Introduction to History." He later returned to Tunis to teach, then wandered off to the Holy Land. In Cairo he became the Supreme Justice of Malakite Law, one of the four rites of Sunni Islam. He died in 1406 in Egypt, but not before interviewing Tamerlane, just as the Mongol warlord's army was about to attack Damascus.

Ibn Khaldun was a free spirit—an adventurous traveler and a shrewd observer. History and geography were subjects he studied on his own, after completing his Islamic education. This helped him avoid theological arguments and empty sophistry in favor of matter-of-fact observation and the grand view. He lived at a time of incipient anarchy: when the Hafsids' hold on northwestern Africa had become precarious, and unrest loomed even in the Hafsid base of Ifriqiyah. The machinations he witnessed among rival tribes and dynasties—a factor behind his own nomadic existence— were so complex as to defy description.

I encountered Ibn Khaldun's *Muqaddimah* before reading Hobbes and Montesquieu: something for which I have been always grateful. That is because his observations about medieval North Africa provide a foundation for understanding the other two philosophers. In fact, as contemporary political science has become increasingly obscurantist, Ibn Khaldun's simple observations of how human beings behave and how climate and geography influence them manifest the clarity of the great works of antiquity, as well as of the Enlightenment. He describes the pattern by which desert nomads, in aspiring to the physical comforts of sedentary life, create the dynamic for urbanization that is then captured by powerful dynasties, which in turn, by providing security, allow cities to flourish. But because royal authority requires luxury, decay sets in, as group solidarity erodes and individuals, through their accumulation of wealth and influence, weaken executive power. Thus, dynasties grow old and die, much as people do.

Ibn Khaldun notes that while luxurious living strengthens the state initially by furthering its legitimacy, in succeeding generations it leads to decadence, with the process of collapse signaled by the rise of powerful provincial governors, who then form their own dynasties. In the latter stages of a dynasty, as order breaks down and attacks on property occur, cultivation is interrupted and famines ensue. He writes, too, about how "partisanship" obscures critical thinking, and about how religious leaders succeed not by calling on God as they claim, but by taking possession of "group feeling," a result of tribe and ethnicity.

Anarchy, he tells us, is the result of the Bedouin not being subdued. Bedouin and tribal identities have always been stronger in Libya and Algeria than in Tunisia. It was Libya's and Algeria's internal disunity that, at the time of my visit, was the underlying cause behind Qaddafi's unruly tyranny and Houari Boumedienne's Soviet-style police state. The *Muqaddimah* provided me with an insight into contemporary North African politics I could never have gleaned from any newspaper.

☙☙

The Bardo, a Hafsid palace rebuilt by a local Turkish dynasty in the seventeenth century, had all the intimacy, clutter, and imperfections of a fine home, even as it was a national museum of classical antiquities. Here was the beauty and crassness of Rome under one dilapidated roof. Mosaics were the Roman Empire's principal art form, with the patterns of tesserae representing order in the universe. There were so many mosaics that I walked over them like carpets. They dated from the third and fourth centuries, a time of Christian martyrdom followed by the triumph of Christianity, and, in turn, by bloody schisms. Rudely sensual faces and forests dripping with grapes and stalked by wild animals imprinted themselves on my memory. Virgil sat in a white toga in one, flanked by the muses of history and tragedy, as though posing for a photograph. The labeling was impossible to read: no matter. The chronology of which civilization and empire and heresy followed which I would become familiar with over the years.

The busts of Roman emperors—Augustus, Vespasian, Trajan, Septimius Severus, Marcus Aurelius, Lucius Verus—made a stronger impression on me here than in the Louvre. To be alone with these distant and arrogant stares as the midday prayer resounded through the archways made me suddenly conscious of Rome *the empire.* It was in Tunisia, more than anywhere else, where Rome had become a world power: a story with which I first became acquainted during a visit to Carthage.

❦

The names of the light-rail stations, decorated in blue-and-white faience, excited my imagination: Carthage Salammbô, Carthage Byrsa, Carthage Hannibal. I found myself repeating the opening words of Flaubert's *Salammbô:* "It was at Megara, a suburb of Carthage, in Hamilcar's gardens. . . ." Megara was now La Marsa, the last stop on the train line.

At the time of my first visit to Tunisia, the northern beach suburbs of Tunis, with their stately white villas backed by dirt roads, still had that half-developed feel of the French Riviera as memorialized in *Tender Is the Night.* Hibiscus and bougainvillea flashed on the walls. Cypresses—nature's answer to mathematical symbols—added a wintry quality to the surroundings. The soil had the rusty orange hue of crushed pottery. Bou Kornein, the "Two-horned Mountain," home of the Phoenician god Baal, shadowed the landscape with disturbing majesty. Loafing on the shore after I had descended from the train at Carthage Salammbô, it was fun to imagine the "cube-shaped" houses, the "yellow-flecked" marble palaces, and "avenues of cypresses" that marked Phoenician Carthage, as described by Flaubert.

In the beginning there were only the Berbers, an Arab corruption of the Greek *barbaroi,* pronounced "Barbary." They were the same indigenous inhabitants that Herodotus called Libyans, a word encompassing all of the peoples of North Africa encountered by the Greeks. The first foreign invasion on these shores came from the Phoenician city-state of Tyre, in the eastern Mediterranean, in 1101 B.C. The

Phoenicians landed twenty-five miles north of here at Utica, a Greek corruption of the Semitic word *atiqa,* meaning "the ancient." At the time, the Phoenicians of Tyre were locked in a struggle with Assyria, and required bases as far west as possible that were safe from Assyrian attack. In 814 B.C., thirty-eight years before the first Olympiad, the Phoenicians moved south to establish the "New City," or Kart Hadshat in their Semitic language, a name that the Romans would corrupt to Carthago. The settlement of Carthage extricated the western Mediterranean from the fog of prehistory: Phoenician Carthage was to become the dominant power in the region, until challenged many centuries later by Rome.

It was the threat posed by this transplanted civilization from the wealthy eastern extremity of the Mediterranean that would encourage the indigenous Berbers to discover themselves as a distinct people. Gradually, the Berbers congealed into the sedentary entities of Numidia and Mauritania (Greek for "Land of the Nomad Shepherds" and "Land of the Moors") that would ceaselessly menace Carthage. This was not unlike the way the Arabs of the Levant gradually developed national identities as "Palestinians," "Jordanians," and so on, as a reaction to the presence of Israel: another highly developed, transplanted civilization.

The founding of Carthage is clothed in sumptuous myth. According to Virgil, King Pygmalion of Tyre craved the wealth of Sychaeus, a high priest married to his sister, Princess Elyssa. Pygmalion had Sychaeus murdered—but his ghost appeared to Elyssa in a dream, telling her to flee Tyre with his treasure before her brother the king could lay his hands on it. So Elyssa sailed with eighty noblemen to

Cyprus, where she collected eighty virgins for the highly respectable task of sacred prostitution. Then she continued to North Africa, or "Libya," by which time she had become known as Dido, Phoenician for "the wanderer." In North Africa she bargained with the Berbers for as much land as could be covered with the skin of a slain ox. Cleverly, she cut the hide into thin strips, which she used to surround an easily defended promontory, known henceforth as Byrsa, a play on words since *byrsa* means "hide" in Greek, while *bosra* is Phoenician for "citadel." As I hiked north along the coast that morning in Carthage, Byrsa Hill loomed on my left.

Thus began a millennium of Semitic civilization on these shores and the nearby steppeland. It was the Phoenicians of Carthage who brought the cultivation of the grape vine and the olive tree from the eastern Mediterranean to North Africa. Nevertheless, for Dido, the first legendary Queen of Carthage, the ending was sad. She committed suicide after being forsaken by her lover, Aeneas, who left her marble bed chamber in order to continue his heroic journey to settle Rome:

> Beating her lovely breast three times, four times,
> And tearing her golden hair,
> > "O Jupiter,"
> She said, "will this man go, will he have mocked
> My kingdom, stranger that he was and is? . . ."

*Infelix Dido,* wrote Virgil: "Unhappy Dido," whose love was spurned. After Aeneas deserted her, she ran herself through with a steel blade atop a burning pyre, as "wails and sobs" echoed through the palace. The truth, as so often is the case, was rather less romantic. Constant tension reigned between the new Phoenician settlers and the local Berbers. Meanwhile, Dido's beauty and intelligence had overwhelmed the Berber chieftain Iarbas, who was not content to vie with other suitors who wanted her for their bride. He said he would exterminate the Carthaginians if she refused him. By taking her life, Dido saved her newly established city.

As Tyre and the other Phoenician city-states of the eastern Mediterranean declined, Carthage grew in influence. Its explorers, like Himilco and Hanno, sailed as far as Brittany and West Africa in the early fifth century B.C. According to Plutarch, the Carthaginians were "a hard and gloomy people, submissive to their rulers and harsh to their subjects. . . ." Though they took delight in their clothes, hair-styles, perfume, jewelry, and confectionary, they took little interest in their bodies. Carthage had no games, no athletes: their gods, unlike those of the Greeks, were always clothed. The men wore beards, skull caps, long sleeves, and were frequently overweight, in Plutarch's caricature. The Phoenician god Baal became their own Baal Hammon, whom they worshiped along with Tanit, his wife. It was said that the temple of Tanit in Carthage was adorned with pygmy skins. In *Salammbô,* the heroine is a priestess of Tanit, who permits a black python, with "eyes more brilliant than carbuncles," to encircle her nude body. Flaubert writes that for the Carthaginians,

> the serpent was both a national and private fetish. It was
> believed to be born of the earth's clay, since it emerged from
> the earth's depths and does not need feet to move over it; its

progress recalled the rippling of rivers, its temperature the ancient, viscous darkness full of fertility, and the circle it describes, as it bites its own tail, the planetary system. . . .

A naturalistic, pre-moral belief system held these people captive. No other gods of pagan antiquity evoke such hideous associations as those of Carthage: it was to appease them in times of trouble that the Carthaginians sacrificed their own children in a burning pit.

The Tophet, the site of child sacrifice in Phoenician Carthage, was a madder-red mulch of broken urns, with moldy stelae sticking crookedly out of the ground. Stick figures of children were carved into the stelae. Plutarch and Diodorus wrote about the child sacrifices here. Though the word *tophet* appears in the Old Testament, it is not known what the Carthaginians themselves called this dreadful place, where the partially cremated remains of children under four years old have been excavated. "They went up slowly," wrote Flaubert,

and as the smoke swirled away in high eddies, they seemed from a distance to be disappearing into a cloud. Not one stirred. They were bound at wrist and ankle, and the somber veils prevented them from seeing anything or being recognized.

These same people dispatched galleys and merchant vessels as far west as the Atlantic, even as gold and other precious metals flowed into Carthage and the rich North African earth yielded up wheat and olive oil. Tanit's temples filled with both riches and the bones of young boys. The destruction of Tyre by the Babylonian Nebuchadnezzar in the first half of the sixth century B.C. eased further Carthage's rise to dominance in the Mediterranean.

Inevitably, Carthage came into conflict with the Greek city-states of nearby Sicily, a conflict that would lead ultimately to a much greater war between Carthage and Rome. War between the Greeks and Carthaginians broke out in 410 B.C. and lasted for over a hundred years, with few pauses. Even by ancient standards, it was merciless. A Carthaginian general had three thousand prisoners tortured and sacrificed in revenge for the death of his grandfather; the Greeks massacred the entire population of Motya, a Phoenician island off the coast of western Sicily. While the Phoenicians of Carthage fought the Greeks of Sicily, to their rear they faced revolts from Berbers in the African interior.

In 310 B.C., toward the end of the hundred-year war with Greek Sicily, Carthage itself was invaded. Agathocles, the dictator of Syracuse in eastern Sicily, landed in Africa with fourteen thousand troops. He lived off the countryside for three years, captured Utica, and plundered the wealthy estates of Carthage. The Carthaginians responded by sacrificing five hundred children of the city's leading families, children known to have been spared on previous occasions when those of slaves had been sacrificed in their place: for the invasion of Agathocles was seen as the revenge of a deceived and angry Tanit.

Agathocles withdrew back across the sea to Syracuse, his invasion frustrated by Berber mercenaries hired by Carthage. But even after his retreat, Greek culture proved too dynamic to be checked. The Phoenicians of Carthage adopted the Greek goddesses of the harvest, Demeter and Persephone, and royal alliances led to intermarriages: Hannibal, the future scourge of Rome, had a Greek mother, and his military use of elephants was learned from Alexander the Great.

As Carthage became more deeply enmeshed in Sicily's affairs, so too did Rome, advancing from the other direction. In the third and second centuries B.C., Sicily became the flashpoint for the three Punic (the Latin word for "Phoenician") Wars: conflicts that would alter the course of history, as well as the global balance of power, to the same degree as World Wars I and II.

The causes of the First Punic War (264–241 B.C.), like those of World War I, were trivial, but were magnified by entangling alliances. A group of Italian colonists in Sicily, nominally Roman citizens, appealed to both Rome and Carthage for help against the Greeks of Syracuse. Because both Rome and Carthage were afraid that the other would use the appeal as a pretext for conquering Sicily, they came to blows. As with America's entry into World War I, it was Rome's first major military venture abroad, and concluded triumphantly with Rome imposing a crushing indemnity upon Carthage— leading, as in the twentieth century, to a second great conflict. The Second Punic War (219–202 B.C.) was the struggle that Livy describes in *The War with Hannibal.* Rome's concessions to Carthage had permitted Hannibal to conquer Spain and southern France, and cross the Alps with elephants into northern Italy before meeting with a response: by which time full-scale war was unavoidable. Like Hitler, who devastated Europe and Russia before withdrawing to the German heartland, Hannibal devastated Italy before being pursued back to Carthage, where the Roman general Scipio routed him decisively a hundred miles southwest of modern-day Tunis.

Nevertheless, tension persisted between Carthage and Rome. The Roman politician Cato made *Carthago delenda est,* "Carthage must be destroyed," his refrain in the Senate. The Third Punic War (149–146 B.C.) saw Rome burn Carthage to the ground, plowing it with salt, making Punic Carthage the Hiroshima of antiquity. Rome now dominated much of the known world, as America did after the Japanese surrender in August 1945.

It was in Tunisia where Rome began to build its empire in earnest. Punic Carthage and Libya were dead; Roman Africa would soon be born. Julius Caesar began the refounding of Carthage in the middle of the first century B.C., believing that native kingdoms were better abolished and Rome was better off with its own established colonies. But his murder in 44 B.C., and the civil war that subsequently divided Rome, interrupted the project. It was Octavian, following his defeat of Mark Antony and Cleopatra in 31 B.C., who demobilized many of his soldiers and sent them to Africa to complete the resettlement of Carthage and establish some two hundred towns. Northern Tunisia became the granary and olive press of the classical world, producing more olive oil than Italy itself. (It still does.) The Romans built thousands of miles of roads, as well as bridges, dams, aqueducts, and irrigation systems. Tunisia became to Rome what India would be to Great Britain, its "jewel in the imperial crown."

Because Punic Carthage had been annihilated, leaving only rubble, it was the remains of a giant Roman bath complex farther along the beach that gave me a glimpse of the spell that Flaubert must have been under during his visit in 1858, the visit that inspired *Salammbô*. Construction had begun under Hadrian and was completed under Antoninus Pius, whose emperorships in the second century A.D. marked the height of Rome's civilizing influence. Vandal, Byzantine, and Arab invasions especially—as well as two millennia of wind and rain—had taken their toll. Towering stone monoliths, their original features eroded, stood now like modern abstractions, as if another hack of the wind would reveal a new face, or some secret. Breakers flooded the marble floor of an adjacent Roman gymnasium. Across the gulf Bou Kornein lay suspended in midday mist, framed in my line of vision between massive Corinthian columns. Because the site was so dramatic and the remains were so minimal, Carthage, writes Michel Zeraffa, was a place of the imagination, a pact made by the sun, the sea, and the lean poetry of stone.

Perched above Byrsa Hill was the Museum of the White Fathers—French Catholic missionaries who had conducted archaeological excavations here in the nineteenth century. In the courtyard I saw a statue of a graceful Roman woman symbolizing victory. Her missing head is rumored to have been lopped off by a Vandal sword. The statue, stained with dark yellow and green mold, stood at the foot of a cypress tree that had sprung from the earth in erect majesty, like Athena from the crown of Zeus. Another headless Roman victory statue stood by an Aleppo pine, and yet another by a

holm oak and a shower of bougainvillea. The sea was cren-
elated by a row of ancient jars and Corinthian capitals.

I smelled dust and flowers rinsed by humid salt air.
Rarely have I felt so alive as I did at that moment, surrounded by mottled Byzantine stone crosses and white marble
sarcophagi. Punic and Roman masks seemed to cry out in
silence. The very incompleteness and disorderliness of the
collection gave it an eccentric, antiquarian quality like that
of a personal library. This Moorish Chatsworth was an inspiration to go on learning, in the elusive hope that its beauty
could somehow be appropriated.

The White Fathers' Museum would later be enlarged and
modernized, and transformed into the National Museum of
Carthage. Here I first became acquainted with the Vandals
and their leader Genseric, who, according to Gibbon, "in the
destruction of the Roman empire has deserved an equal rank
with the names of Alaric and Attila." The Vandals were an
assemblage of Teutonic tribes from Silesia who migrated
south into Pannonia, modern-day Hungary, in the late third
century A.D., at the time of the Roman emperor Aurelian. In
406 A.D. they moved westward across the Rhine into Gaul,
perhaps at the instigation of Stilicho—the last great Roman
military commander in the west. It was Stilicho who used
the Vandals to check the power of other barbarian confed-
erations. Having been defeated in Gaul by the Franks, the
Vandals crossed the Pyrenees. Almost twenty years of war
followed with the Goths and the Suevi before the Vandals
could take possession of Andalusia in southern Spain, from
where they sailed for Africa in 429. By now their leader

Gonderic had died. Leading them across the Strait of Gibraltar was his bastard brother, Genseric.

Genseric was said to be short, lame in one leg from a fall off a horse, and slow in speech. But like Attila the Hun—who only a few years later would ravage the northern borderlands of Rome—Genseric possessed a deep and smoldering ambition, utter ruthlessness, and operational brilliance. While it had taken the Vandals decades to travel from Central Europe to the Atlas Mountains in Morocco, Genseric and his marauding horde of eighty thousand men, women, and children swept across North Africa all the way to Hippo Regius in Numidia (eastern Algeria) in less than a year, their ships hugging the shore alongside them. Ten years later, in 439, Genseric conquered Carthage, and made it the capital of his piratical stronghold. Genseric's Vandal kingdom would eventually stretch a thousand miles across the most fertile part of North Africa, and encompass Sardinia, Corsica, and the Balearic Islands off the coast of Spain. He was the ablest of the barbarian chieftains ever to threaten Rome, which he sacked in 455 before dying peacefully in his bed in Carthage in 477.

In North Africa, Genseric had adopted the Arian heresy, spread the century before by an Alexandrian priest by the name of Arius, who threatened Jesus' divinity by declaring that Jesus was not made of the same substance as God. In this way polytheism was, however vaguely, reintroduced to the Christian world. Many of the Vandal depredations were, in fact, religious persecutions inflicted upon the non-Arian Christians. The worst excesses appear not to have been committed by the Vandals, but by adherents of a particularly puritanical and uncompromising sect, the Donatists, who under cover of Genseric's conquest massacred the other Christians of North Africa.

Despite the eponymous word that they have contributed to our language, the Vandals destroyed less than is supposed in North Africa—the headless statues that I saw notwithstanding. They cut down few olive trees or grape vines, as attested by the Byzantine conquerors who arrived next. Cultivation was the basis of civilization here, which the Vandals prolonged rather than destroyed. The sixth-century Greek historian Procopius writes of their passion for fancy clothes, fine food, and baths, "and all manner of sexual pleasures."

෧෧

Phoenicians carving out a great sovereign state on Berber soil while fending off desert tribesmen: all so that Phoenician Carthage could be culturally infiltrated by the Greeks, and then obliterated by the Romans, whose own imperial longevity would lead to decline and conquest by Vandals . . . The beach at Carthage taught a lesson in the impermanence of empires at a time when the Cold War, and the hegemonic struggle it represented, seemed likely to go on forever.

Of course, given enough centuries all empires decay or transmute into something else. Still, those who struggle hardest affect history the most. The Phoenicians succeeded because they had no doubt about their right to settle wherever they pleased, in pursuit of their own interests. Nor were they intimidated by the indigenous Berbers. Though the Greeks failed at conquering Carthage, the vibrancy of their culture affected the Phoenicians. The Romans were ascendant so long as their civilizing mission inspired them to go out and conquer the world. But when they succumbed to the material pleasures afforded by their own successes, barbarian hordes, while less technologically advanced, saw in Rome something both weak and enticing that they could grab away.

Later that afternoon I visited the American War Cemetery in Carthage, which holds the remains of 2,841 American soldiers killed in the Allied campaigns in North Africa. In November 1942, American troops landed in Morocco to begin the rollback of the Axis powers in the Mediterranean. The Allies retraced the path of the Vandals across North Africa with similar lightning speed. By February 1943, the Americans and British were engaged in tank battles with German Panzer divisions in the Tunisian desert. Tunis and Carthage fell in April, providing, as in antiquity, a staging point for an invasion of Sicily.

Whereas the Romans in their temples and statuary radiate dominance and authority, American war monuments embody a certain chastity and light: as though every cause they fight for is noble. The clipped grass, the neat geranium-lined terraces and gravel trails, the shaped hedgerows, the rectangular marble pylons, and the perfect lines of small white gravestones all spoke of an immaculate harmony. It was as though Washington, D.C., had been transplanted to North Africa, making for an impression far more powerful than in Washington itself. For a moment I felt homesick. As with the Romans, there was a finely engineered quality to everything. Here on the site of Roman Carthage was yet another great civilization that inspired envy.

☾☽

That evening we took a horse and buggy ride for three Tunisian dinars, an extravagance. From the cemetery we took the light-rail farther north to the village of Sidi Bou Said, where for eight dinars we spent the night at a former beylical mansion, the only night that winter that we enjoyed central heating. At dusk we climbed the stairs to the Cafe des Nattes in Sidi Bou Said to drink pine seed tea. The ceiling of our room was decorated with colored glass mirrors and blue faience. Outside in the garden the next morning, I found pink oleanders, orange trees, hibiscus, bougainvillea, and a lone and monumental cypress. I remember the gentle stalking of a cat as a man came by with a broom to sweep the flower petals away.

# 3

## JUGURTHA'S TABLE

The bus trips I made that winter are now a blur in my memory, and my diary provides little help in recapturing the details of individual journeys. But their common features are deeply engraved: the sculpted, liver-hued steppe of northern Tunisia and the pinks of the southern deserts, with their vast blotches of salt; interior tablelands racked by lonely, bone-chilling winds and the grave, museum light of late afternoons; the smoking and hacking coughs of the other passengers wrapped like ghosts in their caftans in the pre-dawn darkness, drooping woolen sleeves concealing their hands; the comforting smell of tea, fresh bread, sharp cheese, and *harissa* at half-empty cafes where the bus stopped after sunrise, with their loud wailing music, scabby walls, and bitter espresso served in whiskey glasses only a third full; the just-boiled eggs that would keep my hands warm in the bus, bought at a cafe or given to me by a friendly passenger with whom I might share my sunflower seeds.

I filled the empty hours learning the Arabic alphabet and writing down new words: *gourbis,* native huts; *ksars,* fortified Berber strongholds; *malafahs,* the head wraps of Tunisian Bedouin women, fastened by silver brooches; Aid el Kebir, the Great Feast of Sacrifice, honoring the story of Abraham and Isaac, which fell on December 15 that year.

ᎧᎧ

Carthage's defeat in the First Punic War—like Germany's in World War I—led to anarchy at home. In Germany's case, troops returned from the front to a destitute country and formed radicalized workers' movements, from which the Nazis emerged. In the case of Carthage, the Berber mercenaries hired by the Carthaginians returned from the battle-front in Sicily to a country that could not afford to pay them for their services, owing, in fact, to the indemnity Carthage had been forced by defeat to pay Rome. The Carthaginians sent the mercenaries and their families to Sicca Veneria, a hundred miles to the west of Carthage, with a gold coin each, and told them to wait there for the balance. But the money did not arrive, and so the mercenaries marched on Carthage. This led to the Mercenary War of 241–238 B.C., which forms the basis of Flaubert's *Salammbô.*

Because the state itself was challenged by an ethnically based mutiny, the general rules of war were ignored. Each side knew that whoever lost would be annihilated. Cartha-

ginians captured by the mercenaries were dismembered and
thrown into burning ditches, while captured mercenaries
were trampled by elephants. The war ended only when a
Numidian tribe deserted to the Carthaginians, allowing the
Carthaginians to destroy the other mercenaries.

The road westward to Sicca Veneria led through olive
tree plantations bordered by rows of prickly pears. In one
place, the mercenaries gasped at a line of crosses on which
local peasants had crucified lions in an attempt to scare off
other beasts. The mercenaries marched for seven days, the
landscape growing drier and gradually shedding its greenery
as they receded farther from the capital.

Several hours on a bus along a road lined with military
milestones brought me to Tebersouk, halfway to Sicca Veneria. Tebersouk was a ramshackle town on a scraped hillside
with muddy lanes. Men wore soggy brown caftans and the
women had tribal tattoos. The hike from Tebersouk to the
Roman ruins at Dougga is three miles. I forget how long
the walk took, but I remember the line of burnt-sienna ridges
floating above green cereal fields. As the ruins appeared, I saw a
man sitting cross-legged on a donkey, draped in a long caftan
and white sheet like a hooded figure in a medieval landscape.

The mass of ruins stood on a remote and spooky hillside:
the yelps of wild dogs and the tinkle of sheep bells were the
only sounds for miles. A shepherd in a beret and trench coat
asked me for a cigarette. Given the site's isolation, he seemed
just another ghostly apparition. His sheep sauntered through
the temples, forums, and bath complex with their jangling
bells like a marauding army of time, before passing out of

sight under the arch of Septimius Severus, Rome's first African-born emperor. As the sun prowled in and out of somber clouds, the ruins turned every shade of ocher. The columns, pediments, and bas-reliefs were so smooth, as if they had been baked and polished in a kiln. From inside the Temple of Minerva, I looked down on a Roman theater that seemed suspended above swirling, olive-striped valleys no different from those through which the mercenaries had passed.

The inscriptions were in Berber, Phoenician, Greek, and Latin, commemorating a cosmopolitan culture that had lasted a thousand years. By the end of the fourth century B.C., Dougga (ancient Thugga) was already a Berber city of "fine size," according to Diodorus. In the late second century B.C., it became the official residence of Massinissa, the Numidian king. The population was then a mixture of native Berbers and Carthaginians. Later a monumental Roman city was built here, and populated with Latin settlers; it thrived until the fourth century A.D.

Rome's conquest of Africa had occurred in stages. After Scipio had defeated Hannibal in the steppes near Dougga in 202 B.C., he dug a demarcation ditch, a *fossa regia,* that marked the extent of Carthaginian territory. The ditch is still visible in places. It starts at the Mediterranean port of Tabarka, near Tunisia's western border with Algeria, then heads south into the desert before veering east to reach the Mediterranean again at Sfax. Following Rome's annihilation of Carthage, Julius Caesar began extending Rome's political authority beyond the demarcation ditch: the territory inside the ditch became known as Africa Vetus, or "Old Africa," and the territory outside as Africa Nova, "New Africa." Rome ruled Africa Nova through its Numidian kings. When that proved ineffective, the entire region was made a colony under direct Roman rule. Both Africa Vetus and Africa Nova were thereafter called Africa Proconsularis.

Roman colonization manifested itself in a dense network of roads and aqueducts that would eventually connect six hundred cities from Volubilis in present-day Morocco to Leptis Magna in Libya. It was comparable to the infrastructure built by the British to unite the Indian subcontinent. The greatest concentration of these cities—some two hundred—lay in the northern third of Tunisia, the most fertile part of North Africa. Gibbon writes: "The long and narrow tract of the African coast was filled with frequent monuments of Roman art and magnificence; and the respective degrees of improvement might be accurately measured by the distance from Carthage. . . ."

The closer to Carthage, the greater the development. Roman hydraulic works opened up new areas of cultivation as nomadism declined. Ibn Khaldun observed that the conversion of nomads to sedentary life is the first step in building cities and states. In northern Tunisia, where the bulk of Tunisians live today, that process began with the Romans two thousand years ago. The open pastures through which the mercenaries passed in Carthaginian times had become a ribbon of towns spaced six miles apart at the apex of Roman occupation.

Modern Tunisia was the outgrowth of that legacy. It was a well-governed country, crisscrossed by good roads built

over the original Roman ones. Bus travel was safe everywhere, a large middle class existed despite the absence of oil
(a rarity for the Arab world), and people argued about the
budget and food subsidies, not about the extremist ideologies
that preoccupied neighboring Algeria and Libya. Tunisia had
a national culture; it was not a collection of tribes.

Jutting out into the center of the Mediterranean close to
Sicily, Tunisia had been the hub of North Africa not only
under the Carthaginians and Romans, but under the Vandals, Byzantines, Arabs, and Turks, too. In the 1850s, the
Husseinite dynasty here was the first in the Arab world to
ban slavery and draw up a constitution. Unlike Algeria,
Tunisia wrested its independence from France in 1956 with
little bloodshed. For decades thereafter, Tunisia's president,
Habib Bourguiba, was the most enlightened and secular
ruler in the Moslem world. With the legitimacy of the state
deeply rooted in antiquity, there was no need to spend
money on grandiose building projects: generous portions of
the budget were devoted to rural women's literacy, birth
control, and primary-school education.

Contrarily, Algeria and Libya had virtually no history as
organized states prior to the arrival of nineteenth-century
colonial mapmakers: they were not nations so much as vague
geographical expressions. The ancient cities of Thagaste and
Hippo Regius in eastern Algeria were oriented toward
Carthage, just as the cities of western Algeria were linked to
the venerable Berber kingdoms of Morocco. The cities of
western Libya, such as Leptis Magna and Sabratha near the
modern-day capital of Tripoli, also fell within the orbit of
Carthage, even as the towns of eastern Libya looked toward

Alexandria and the Nile. Tunisia, like Morocco and Egypt, constituted an age-old civilization cluster. It did not require a radical ideology to mobilize its population and keep order.

That winter I learned that history forms the starting point for whatever drama happens to be occurring at any time, anywhere. Indeed, the predicament of modern Tunisia had its roots in antiquity. Just as the settled farmers of Carthage and Roman Africa were threatened by the semi-nomadic pastoralists of Numidia, the threat of radicalism seeping over the borders from Algeria and Libya was the dominant fear at the time in Tunisia.

Scipio's *fossa regia* was still a reality. Continuing west-ward toward Sicca Veneria from Tebersouk, I looked out the bus window and saw a coppery landscape of sharp, cresting hills where the greenery had been reduced to pale stubble fields. Beyond the Roman demarcation ditch, in Tunisia's western and southern outbacks, I confronted poorer and more traditional towns, where the bus stations had no posted time-tables and unemployment was ubiquitous judging by the throngs of men hanging about cafes. Here Tunisia was more like the rest of North Africa and less a continuation of southern Europe. The government made special efforts to integrate the far west and the south beyond the demarcation ditch by building roads, telephone lines, and other infra-structure. "In Roman times you could ignore the periphery, today we need to draw in the shadow zone beyond Roman settlement that is within our borders," the minister of culture, Abdelbaki Hermassi, would tell me on a later visit.

Sicca Veneria was originally a Carthaginian town famous for its pagan temple, where prostitutes could always be found. Flaubert writes that on the last day of their march, the mercenaries "suddenly turned to the right; then a line of walls came into sight, set upon white rocks . . . the whole town rose up; blue, yellow, and white veils waved on the walls, in the red evening glow. It was the priestesses of Tanit who had run to welcome the men." The Romans rededicated the temple to Venus—hence the name, Sicca Veneria. The Arabs simply called it Le Kef, "the Rock," because the houses tumbled down from a dramatic bluff.

From the ramparts of the Turkish Kasbah atop the bluff where Carthaginian, Roman, and Byzantine forts had stood, I could see deep into Algeria over a rib-work of hills so gaunt it seemed the wind had torn the flesh off them. The late-afternoon winter light bathed it all in a dreary darkness. In the distance I could make out Jugurtha's Table, a giant mesa forty-five miles to the southwest by the Algerian border, its summit so flat—and its walls so perfectly sheer—it looked man-made. The mesa was named after a Numidian king who had used the summit as a base for his war against the Romans from 112 to 105 B.C. Here in this austere back-of-beyond never conquered by the Latin language, Rome fought one of those thankless counter-insurgency campaigns with which all great powers are familiar.

The conflict is described in *The Jugurthine War,* one of the great literary works of antiquity, composed by Sallust, a writer of histories who also served the Roman Republic in its last days. Following Rome's subjugation of Numidia, Sallust was appointed by Julius Caesar as the first Roman governor of Africa Nova. It was a reward for his loyalty in standing with Caesar against Caesar's rival, Pompey. Sallust's governorship gave him the opportunity to compile material for an account of a war that had occurred seventy years earlier. I found Sallust easy to read. His style is spare and elegant, free of the jargon of the many academic texts I had been forced to consume in college.

Sallust's story begins with King Massinissa, the first great Berber figure in recorded history—the same Massinissa who made Dougga his official residence. Toward the end of the Second Punic War, as Scipio was on the verge of defeating Hannibal, the young Massinissa had come to Rome's aid against the Carthaginians, even though it had meant annulling his marriage to a beautiful Carthaginian princess. The princess, Sophonisba, subsequently drank a cup of poison, while Massinissa went on to a long and successful career as king of Numidia and ally of Rome. When he died, his son Micipsa inherited the throne. Micipsa had two sons. But a third boy also grew up in the palace, the illegitimate son of Micipsa's late brother who had died of disease. That boy was Jugurtha.

The "bastard" Jugurtha was stronger, handsomer, and smarter than Micipsa's two sons. Aware of the threat he posed to the succession, Micipsa sent Jugurtha to Spain to fight alongside Roman forces, in the hope that he would be killed. But Jugurtha returned a mean and hardened warrior. Following Micipsa's death, Jugurtha murdered Hiempsal, one of Micipsa's sons. The other son, Adherbal, fled to Rome to plead for help against the usurper. But Jugurtha was clever and sent bribes to key Roman officials. Rome decided to divide Numidia, giving Jugurtha the richer, western half and

Adherbal the poorer, eastern one. Soon after, Jugurtha attacked Adherbal and took eastern Numidia. This might all have passed unnoticed were it not for the fact that a number of Italian merchants had been killed in Jugurtha's assault, igniting popular rage in Rome and forcing the Senate to declare war.

The Roman expeditionary force languished in the stony hills and thickets of Numidia. Jugurtha would burn the grass and contaminate the springs in the territory through which the Romans were about to pass, after which he would surround them on adjacent hills and bribe their commanders to cease fighting. "For Jugurtha was so crafty," writes Sallust, "so well acquainted with the country, and so experienced in warfare, that one never knew which was the more deadly— his presence or his absence, his offers of peace or his threats of hostilities." In 110 B.C., Jugurtha forced the capitulation of an entire Roman army. But Rome was too certain of itself to admit defeat. It dispatched a new commander, Gaius Marius, a plebian who had risen through the ranks in a military career that began in Spain, but Jugurtha's guerrilla tactics stymied him too. Still, Marius would not give up. First, he led his troops on plundering expeditions to gather corn and other provisions, then forced-marched them through paths hidden behind hills in the desert, and burnt and sacked Numidian towns. This put Marius in a position to convince the Mauretanian king Bocchus to enter into an alliance of convenience with Rome. It was Bocchus who invited Jugurtha to a peace conference in 105 B.C., where he was trapped and handed over to the Romans. Jugurtha was executed the following year.

Toward the end of the war, according to Sallust, Jugurtha "had lost all his friends, most of whom he had himself put to death, while the rest in their fear had taken refuge either with the Romans or with King Bocchus." Jugurtha "changed his officers and his marching orders from day to day, first advancing against the enemy in the hope of victory, then seeking to save himself by retreating into the desert . . . he had as little confidence in the courage of his subjects as he had in their loyalty." It had been a war of informers, where one feared one's own soldiers as much as the enemy. Jugurtha slept in a different hideout each night, changing his mind, procrastinating. Over the years, I would see elements of Jugurtha in Manuel Noriega, Saddam Hussein, Osama bin Laden, and others who challenged America's imperial authority. Jugurtha had been misled into believing that because Rome's policy was often clumsy and ambivalent, and its governing class weakened by corruption and partisanship, the empire would not respond with force if its interests were threatened.

Decades later, on a return visit to Tunisia, I climbed halfway to the summit of Jugurtha's Table. It was late afternoon on New Year's Eve day and I was alone. Jugurtha's Table would turn out to be the coldest and most hostile place I would visit in Tunisia, overlooking a tundra-like plateau with only a grim border village nearby. The sky was the color of steel tinged with charcoal. All around were knife-like, coffee-brown depressions. The scene manifested an uncompromising minimalism. I felt dissected by the wind, which had emptied the landscape of everything but its past.

From the ramparts of the Kasbah on my first visit to Le

Kef I had headed downhill through the town. On that day, too, the wind was savage, as it often is here in winter. Eucalyptus trees groaned; a large branch snapped and smashed a car. I took refuge in a bare-walled restaurant and finished a *casse-croûte* and Coke. My fingers stained with olive oil, I went out into the street, where it had started to rain. I almost slipped several times on the flagstones and fled into a small Byzantine church, empty except for an antique jar on a table in the apse.

When the rain had stopped I emerged like a hermit crab from my shell and took in my surroundings. Nearby was a mosque whose cruciform design indicated it had been a church in Byzantine times, prior to the Arab invasion. A few women in ruby head wraps and silver tribal jewelry were burning incense and brewing tea in the middle of the prayer hall by the tomb of an Islamic holy man, their children playing on the worn mats. The women laughed quietly as I tested my Arabic with them. The whole place had a distinctly pagan feel. I felt myself within some kind of magical chamber, where the spirits of paganism, Christianity, and Islam were whirling about: where classical antiquity and the tribal world of the Berbers had fused with monotheistic religions. This was the world of St. Augustine, a Berber born in 354 A.D. in Thagaste (Souk Ahras), an hour's journey to the west inside Algeria. St. Augustine's philosophy fuses pagan Rome and early Christianity: it has to be *tasted,* not merely read.

When Augustine writes about "vintages" and the "spacious structures of memory," he is betraying his sensuous past. The mountains and steppeland of North Africa sustained his spirit, and gave it its unyielding edge. For St. Augustine, this hardy terrain symbolized God's austere permanence; while the sea, where he had once endured a storm en route to Italy, meant chaos. His haunting, aromatic monologues and rigorous philosophy—in which he subjects Christianity to the logic of Plato and Cicero—was an outgrowth of this tough and restrained landscape.

Augustine was an impatient intellectual, a searcher, a dabbler. His favorite poem was Virgil's *Aeneid*. In Carthage, where he came to live as a seventeen-year-old, he consorted with street toughs and helped raise an unwanted child he had fathered. There, and later in Rome and Milan, he drifted from pagan philosophy to Manichaeism and finally to Christianity—going from one circle of thinkers to another—the way an intellectual today might move from Marxism to liberalism to neoconservatism. He craved the "spice" and "dissent" of late-night arguments. He describes heated discussions among beloved friends as "separate sparks" fusing "into a single glow, no longer many souls, but one."

Augustine's vagabond experiences as a youth, and his later forays on the front lines of the bloody schisms that racked the African borderlands of Rome in the fourth and fifth centuries, made him appreciate that the difference between saints and sinners was vaguer than we think; that one could be a sinner in one phase of life and a saint the next (as he had been); that society requires both kinds of men; that it puts up with irrational tribalism just as it does enlightened thought. He was an observer to a degree that other theologians were not. At times, his descriptions of men and their conflicts are closer to Ibn Khaldun's than to those of other Christian saints. In *The City of God,* written after the Visigoth Alaric had sacked Rome in 410 A.D., Augustine observes that society is based on hard social compromises rather than on theories of perfect justice: that civic life is more suited to "the remission of sins than the perfection of virtues."

Augustine felt that Adam's original sin of eating the forbidden fruit had an understandable purpose. It was to preserve his bond of companionship with Eve: the search for love of others leads us away from the love of God. Nevertheless, as Augustine explains, it is the things we love in common, including our love for each other, that form the basis of healthy politics. Augustine's philosophy helped me appreciate Rodin's art. Both show human beings in the earthly world after the Fall, where suffering and conflict are unavoidable.

Augustine's acknowledgment of human conflict owes a great deal to his own battles with various Christian heresies that flared here before being snuffed out under the blanket of Islam. There was something about this bare and undefiled landscape that encouraged zeal. At the end of the third century there was an ardent teacher of pagan rhetoric in Le Kef, Arnobius, who converted to Christianity and henceforth became a fiery orator against his earlier paganism.

In North Africa, Christianity was a religion of the poor. It took root at first in the cities and then spread to the countryside. Because it was a religion of the uneducated, it bore much of the superstition of the paganism it had displaced. Just as the Carthaginian god Baal Hammon (who had evolved into the Roman Saturn-Baal) embodied a vengeful cult of death, so did the Donatist heresy against which

Augustine railed. Its rabble-rousing founder, Donatus, had emerged from the bleak salt beds, or *chotts,* in the desert south of Le Kef, where he stirred crowds and gathered support. Donatism drew its fire from the Great Persecution ordered by the Roman emperor Diocletian in 303–305 A.D., only eight years before Constantine made Christianity the church of Rome. Following decades of weak emperors, Diocletian restored strong executive authority to North Africa and increased the size of Rome's frontier army. Donatism was the populist reaction to this renewal of direct Roman rule. It threatened the sacramental aspect of Christianity by holding that only priests of perfect character could be agents of God during the mass. The Donatists' distrust of human nature, especially that of priests, arose out of their experience during the persecutions, when they had seen many good Christians yield under the pressure of extreme circumstances. At one time, Donatism claimed the support of half of North Africa's Christians. It was a radical movement that worshiped the martyrs of Diocletian at special shrines where relics were sold and miracles were said to take place. Donatists cultivated a stubborn and hateful memory of those who had betrayed the Christian martyrs. They staged riots in Carthage that were suppressed by Roman troops, and used the opportunity of the Vandal invasion to murder orthodox Christians. Augustine's experience of them allowed him to admire some Donatist thinkers, even as he sanctioned violence against them when softer measures failed.

Augustine died at the age of seventy-six in 430 A.D., in the midst of the assault of Genseric's Vandals on Africa Proconsularis. His death, along with the collapse of the Western

Roman Empire in 476, commonly marks the beginning of the Middle Ages.

The new Vandal rulers of Africa coexisted for a while with a rising Eastern Roman Empire, headquartered in Constantinople. But in the early sixth century, the Byzantine emperor Justinian, taking advantage of dynastic squabbles in Carthage among Genseric's successors, ordered the invasion of Vandal Africa. Thereafter, the Byzantines ruled Africa from afar, ruining it financially. The Roman fortresses they repaired in Le Kef and elsewhere were mere redoubts against growing tribal anarchy. Meanwhile, Donatism continued to flourish in the rural interior until the seventh century, when Mohammed's armies crushed it definitively.

From Le Kef, I traveled through the frontier zone of the original Africa Vetus, visiting ruined cities on either side of Scipio's demarcation ditch, where, as in antiquity, the human and physical surroundings suddenly became more rugged. At Bulla Regia, amid red limestone hills, fifty miles to the north of Le Kef, my guide wore a woolen ski cap and a tattered cape. He led me briskly down an avenue of third- and fourth-century Roman flagstones in the midst of literally nowhere. Jangling open a gate at the bottom of a few steps, we entered an underground marble colonnade. Because Bulla Regia ("Site of Royalty," a reference to the Numidian kings who predated the Romans) suffered infernal summers and wet winters, its Roman colonists built their villas beneath the surface. The floor of this particular mansion was a carpet of mosaics, the pinks of fatty bodies clashing with their smoky backgrounds. Augustine had come to Bulla Regia to fulminate against its sensuality and materialism. The rain of the previous night had submerged some of the mosaics beneath puddles. My guide grabbed a filthy sponge, dipped it into the brown water, and began scrubbing away mud from the knowing face of Venus, whom Cupid was admiring in a mirror.

I was not far from Chemtou, where the Romans at the time of Jesus began quarrying for marble. After imperial porphyry, the marble here was the most expensive in the empire. It was exported as far west as Iberia and as far east as Asia Minor, each block bearing the stamp of the emperor. Thousands of slaves worked the Chemtou mines for seven centuries before the Arab invasion. Chemtou was now deserted, and the wind so resolute that it forced me back into a hut, where the guard on duty was brewing tea.

I relished the bad weather. Like the smell of mint in the simmering tea, there was an intimacy to it. I burrowed inside coarse blankets and a sleeping bag in unheated hotel rooms with bare cement walls. The boiled eggs and tea in the morning—followed by a whiskey-shot's worth of coffee—was something to look forward to. Warmer days would bring out other tourists, and I wanted the past to myself.

Maktar and Zama lay south of Le Kef across limestone lunar uplands and dark grain fields.

Maktar: another town whose streets and plazas had been filled for a thousand years from the time of the Carthaginians. Now it was a picture of desolation—scarred heads of Roman emperors, shattered columns, winged remnants of crumbled walls—the gray flagstone pavement of the forum imitating the limitless vastness above. That winter I acquired the habit of never using a camera. It forced me to work harder, writing down every detail. Photographs can be passive and reductive. They allow us to recall too easily, omitting from view what is behind the camera, and to the sides of it.

Zama: the site of the battle in 202 B.C. between Scipio and Hannibal that ended the Second Punic War. Here, a century later, Jugurtha exhorted the townspeople to defend their walls against the Romans. That was shortly before he marched to Le Kef, where he attacked the Romans from the rear. Zama commanded the strategic heights of north-central Tunisia. It overlooked a plateau so austere it seemed to have the consistency of marble. In the purer sunlight of this high elevation, particularly after it rained, the shepherds and their flocks had the archetypal quality of Homeric myth. The "baaa" of reddish-brown Barbary sheep pierced the thin air like prayer calls. Beyond a jigsaw of Roman and Byzantine foundations there was little to see. There were no signs, no facilities; only one bad road.

Then there was Sbeitla, known to the Romans and Byzantines as Sufetula. Sbeitla lay seventy miles south of Le Kef on the southern edge of Africa Proconsularis. I remember bus stations caked with mud where men with whiskery beards, their eyes concealed beneath hooded caftans—cigarettes dangling from red, henna-stained fingers—sat sideways on broken chairs in the station cafes. I saw boys with checkered *keffiyahs* wrapped across their faces to protect them from the dusty wind—this was more than a decade before the first Palestinian Intifada made the style famous. Near Sbeitla the steppe began its granular decline into a sandy desert, which farther south would become known as the Sahara. It was here that General George Patton's tank units first engaged Rommel's Afrika Corps in late 1942. It was here too that Byzantium made its last stand against Arab invaders, bringing the Roman legacy in Africa to an end.

In the winter of 1975–76, the town of Sbeitla had yet to expand to its present size. There were only the remains of a Roman-Byzantine city sprinkled over the stony wilderness, accessible only by foot from the town a mile away. From the vantage point of a millennium and a half, the Byzantine-era churches appeared to me little different from the Roman-era pagan temples. Both belonged to a classical civilization distinct from the medieval Islamic one that was to replace them.

In 641 A.D., less than a decade after the Prophet Mohammed's death, Arab armies conquered Egypt. In 642, they conquered Cyrenaica in present-day eastern Libya. In 643 they plundered Leptis Magna and Sabratha in western Libya. Aware that Carthage would be next, and seeing no help on the way, the Byzantine prefect Gregory secured the support of Berber chieftains and in 647 moved the capital of Africa Proconsularis from Carthage to Sbeitla, 160 miles to the southwest. Sbeitla was a Roman city, secluded and surrounded by olive groves, that had remained prosperous long after other Roman cities in the region had declined. The Arab siege of Sbeitla lasted several months until Gregory's forces were overrun. Gregory was killed in battle. His daughter, who fought alongside him, committed suicide

rather than be taken back to Egypt. Ever since the Phoenicians had landed at Utica nearly eighteen centuries before,
Tunisia had been dominated by cultures from the sea. Henceforth, it would be dominated by a force that had emerged
from the desert. Roman-Byzantine Africa would become a
new Arab-Moslem Ifriqiyah.

## · 4 ·

# PAUL KLEE'S ISLAMIC ABSTRACTIONS

As December wore on, we continued south into the desert, where sand and fleas blew into a succession of frigid rooms. Gafsa lay seventy miles south of Sbeitla. Here in 107 B.C., having marched for three successive nights, the Romans under Marius took Jugurtha's forces by surprise. The town was now a collection of cinder block buildings as forlorn as any of the ancient ruins. All around were faded reeds known as halfa grass, and bleached gray hillsides seemingly chewed by primordial teeth. "A blizzard is raging that would flay a rhinoceros," reported the Scottish traveler Norman Douglas during a visit to Gafsa in January 1912. He recommended "Arctic vestment" for the winter here, which we did not have. So we slept in our clothes, when they weren't damp.

But there were warm and sunny days too, when the sky was free of dust. I recall glittering mountains of blood oranges and piles of dates in the sprawling oases southwest of Gafsa, the latter fruit cultivated by the ancient Egyptians as early as 3000 B.C. and mentioned by the Greco-Egyptian geographer Ptolemy, the first classical writer to describe this region. I won't forget the thick masses of camels we would be forced to give way to crossing the road, or the honeycombed *gourbis* inhabited by peasants and poor laborers since time immemorial, rising from the earth like filthy air bubbles.

There were the *chotts,* cracked depressions of encrusted salt that stretched up to sixty miles, by whose awful standard even the desert was guilty of ostentation. "They are fringed by a light so intense that it is a relief to look up at the sky," writes the traveler Michel Zeraffa. The *chotts* formed the backdrop for the early sermons of Donatus, who took his extremist vision north from here. According to some legends, they are also the birthplace of Poseidon, Perseus, and Medusa. "Unlike the living ocean," writes Norman Douglas, "this withered one never smiles: it wears a hostile face. There is a charm, none the less—a charm that appeals to complex modern minds—in that picture of eternal, irremediable sterility." André Gide, who visited North Africa at the same time, felt a similar emotion when he heard the four-holed desert flute: "what subtle diversity I taste in your monotony."

But it was the Swiss artist Paul Klee who wrested the richest memories from the seemingly irreducible abstractions of the Tunisian desert. In April 1914, Klee spent twelve days in Tunisia that changed his art forever. In the Islamic holy city of Kairouan, he became a modernist—painting in symbols to convey the essential spiritual significance of the natural world. On April 15, he arrived in Kairouan and wrote in his diary that the place was "penetrating . . . intoxicating . . . clarifying." The next morning he painted the city from the desert just outside the gates, writing,

> a gently diffused light falls, at once mild and clear. . . . It penetrates so deeply and so gently into me, I feel it and it gives me confidence in myself without effort. Color possesses me. I don't have to pursue it. It will possess me always, I know it. That is the meaning of this happy hour: Color and I are one. I am a painter.

The day he wrote those words proclaiming his discovery of color, he painted "Before the Gates of Kairouan," which shows a cityscape disintegrating into a patchwork of delicate, watery hues, the only recognizable objects a white dome and three small horses. This painting marks Klee's transition to abstract art. (A similar evolution can be traced in the work of Russian painter Wassily Kandinsky after his visit to Tunisia in 1904.) Henceforth, Klee would rely on color to depict his own interior universe. To Klee, accustomed to the baroque patterns of northern Europe, the brilliant light and clean, severe architecture of Kairouan revealed a pellucid harmony he had not known before.

☯

Only thirty-six miles inland from the Mediterranean, Kairouan is wholly of the desert. The warrior Okba ben Nafi founded Kairouan in 670 A.D., three years after Sbeitla had fallen; it was the first major Islamic encampment in North Africa. The name Kairouan means "arsenal" or "camp-site." It was far enough from the coastal waters patrolled by the Byzantine fleet to provide a modicum of safety, and out of reach of the unruly Berbers deeper in the interior, whom Okba would later convert after massacring and enslaving the Christians. Built from the unbaked stones that littered the plain, Kairouan rose as a monument to the sword and to the Koran. With eighty-nine mosques it is the fourth holiest city in Sunni Islam, after Mecca, Medina, and Jerusalem. A tradition holds that seven pilgrimages to Kairouan exempt the faithful from having to journey to Mecca. Kairouan struck me as a fairy-tale version of Mecca: dipped in a pool of white paint and laid out to dry in the glaring desert sun, draped with carpets over its sky-blue doors, and studded with minarets.

Even after a quarter of a century, the Great Mosque of Kairouan is still the most impressive building I have seen in the Arab world. I learned more from walking around its court-yard and prayer hall, and sitting quietly beneath its teeming forest of columns, than from many of the books about Arab civilization that I have read since. The Great Mosque illus-trates why journalism must sometimes be done silently: to know the character of a people, observe what they build.

The Great Mosque emerged out of Roman and Byzan-tine military architecture and became a prototype of North African Islamic architecture. It is the equivalent in stone of Augustine's philosophy: fusing the sensibilities of the classi-cal and medieval worlds. Like the walls topped by jagged glass that conceal sumptuous homes throughout the Middle

East, the Great Mosque is a Romanesque fort, terrifying in its solemnity, that screens a paradise within.

Islam was founded upon rapid military advance. It is a religion that harbors no doubts: it is always prepared to fight. This introverted sanctuary perfectly expresses that principle.

The Great Mosque was built and rebuilt throughout the eighth and ninth centuries by the Omayyad and Aghlabid rulers dispatched from Syria and Mesopotamia as the numbers of the faithful continued to swell and Kairouan replaced Carthage as the political and cultural center of North Africa. The two-meter-thick battlements, in their angular perfection, seemed in the freezing, dust-lashed winter wind especially hostile. The minaret, a squat pylon capped by a ribbed tulip dome, radiated dominion. The colonnades of the quadrangular courtyard—sloping inward to collect rainwater in underground cisterns—imparted a sensation of space and infinity.

The prayer hall, with its Venetian chandeliers, had the impersonal grandeur of a European train station. The panels of Greek marble had been carved in Mesopotamia, the Corinthian capitals had been ransacked by the Arab conquerors from the ruins of Carthage. Pendentives supported domes, glorifying a planetary system that rested on crushing, absolute truths.

Kairouan was a hotbed of orthodoxy, not of fundamentalism. Pockets of Islamic extremism would later emerge from the slums around Tunis, where migrants from the countryside reinvented religion in a more ideological form to protect them from the temptations of pseudo-western urban life. But Kairouan back then was small enough so that every-one knew each other. It was stifling and conservative, but not radical.

The Mosque of the Barber holds the tomb of Abu Zam'a Ubayd al-Arquam al Balawi, known also as Sidi Saheb, killed in 654 A.D. not far from here on one of the early Moslem military expeditions to Ifriqiyah. Back in Arabia he had been a companion of the Prophet Mohammed, and was said to travel with three hairs of the Prophet's beard. The mosque that honored him was testament to Ottoman and Andalusian ostentation, which the Great Mosque purpose-fully repudiated. As we entered the courtyard, the cries of birds darting through the Moorish archways competed with the booming voice of Khalil, who had taken it upon himself to be our guide.

"This is holy water," Khalil thundered, pointing to a scented liquid encased in the corner of a magnificent white stucco wall, punctuated with splashy orange, green, and blue faience. "No, no, you may not touch it. It is only for Musul-mans!" Khalil wore a tattered overcoat and a pink-and-white towel around his neck. "And in that chamber are the remains of Sidi Saheb, friend of the Prophet Mohammed," he contin-ued. "No, no, you cannot go in, it is only for Musulmans! But for one dinar, it is possible for you." The floor, walls, and tomb were shrouded under rugs woven by local women, who have for centuries been donating the first carpet they make as a child to this mausoleum. I saw women bundled in dazzling red and purple robes praying on the floor alongside noisy children. Fluorescent lights illuminated the Andalusian tiles and stuccoed walls. I felt as though I were inside a giant, twisting kaleidoscope. The perspiring crowd squeezed against me. "You must go every day to the mosque, every day you must go," Khalil implored. As we left the mosque and courtyard, his voice lifted above the wind rolling up dust clouds into the eucalyptus branches.

The next morning we walked through winding white passageways to Khalil's house. I remember the cracked blue portico strung with dusty red pimentos. Hearing our footsteps, Khalil met us at the door, hoisting his palms heavenward in an arc. "Welcome, my friends," he said gently now, "welcome."

We entered a whitewashed courtyard leading to a long room painted milky blue with a dirt floor. An old woman with tattoos, little more than a fragile bundle of red robes, sat hunched over a ceramic bowl, shelling nuts. A girl worked the iron comb of a carpet loom, tightening the row of stitches she had just made. Thick eyebrows connected across the bridge of her nose. Her expression was old and beaten, though she was probably still in her teens. She turned her face away when Khalil introduced her as his wife. A little naked boy banged his heels against the floor and screamed: it was his son. "You will eat soon," Khalil told us, picking up the boy and making funny faces at him. The old tattooed woman, Khalil's mother, disappeared into the kitchen. I noticed a mirror in a purple plastic frame on the wall, and stiff black-and-white photographs of Khalil's family on a Formica dresser.

Lunch was a *brik* (pastry with a fried egg inside), yogurt, lamb, semolina flavored with hot red peppers, and mint tea. Khalil pointed to the semolina and roared: "Eat, eat." It was the only thing he said as he stared intently at us throughout the meal. Following a dessert of almonds and mandarins came another solicitation: would we like to visit the Turkish baths? My companion went with Ruah, Khalil's wife. I went to the men's baths with Khalil.

Steam rose within a circle of painted columns. A man doused me with jasmine-scented water and scrubbed me with a bristled glove. I remember the copper kettles with long nozzles that Khalil used for pouring tea when we sat in one of the cooling chambers. Khalil accompanied me back to our hotel. Then he asked if he could come upstairs to our room. I told him that I was tired, but that we could all meet again tomorrow. Annoyance swept across his face. "Why do all you Europeans play games with me?" he exploded. I was suspicious and confused as we faced each other in the street, full of embarrassment. Khalil was a tourist tout and our relationship with him had been full of cliches. Perhaps he had only wanted me to return his hospitality by inviting him to our small room. Or perhaps he had wanted something else. It was such superficial and misconstrued encounters that, in an age of increased travel, were part of the Moslem world's exposure to the West and ours to the Moslem world. Over the years, whenever I saw the angry faces of young Arab men on television, protesting some indignity or perceived one, I thought of Khalil and our misunderstanding.

໐໐

The next morning I was on a fly-beaten bus, crossing the width of the Tunisian Sahel, an oceanic wilderness dipping downward to the sea with an occasional donkey silhouetted against the broad sky, laden with clay jugs. The other passengers were Zlass tribesmen, with tattoos, garish robes, and gold bangles. A half hour later, the first rows of olive trees signaled that the Mediterranean was nearby. The Romans began cultivating olives in this semi-desert because the olive tree required even less water than the palm tree.

Forty-five minutes after leaving Kairouan with its throngs of veiled women, I was sitting at an outdoor cafe in Sousse, sipping a cappuccino and gazing at a beach where Europeans were sunbathing in bikinis. Tunisia was a schizoid clash of insular desert and cosmopolitan harbors. The unease that I had felt in Kairouan dissolved upon arrival in Sousse, making me conscious for the first time of my own cultural fears. At the post office in Sousse, I picked up my first-ever free-lance check: $40 from the *Christian Science Monitor* for a travel article I had written about Sidi Bou Said. I was ecstatic for days, when I began thinking about the next article, and the next check.

Sousse's *medina* is dramatically situated on a hill that overlooks the sea, the harbor, and the train station. Strolling the alleyways, I watched a ship sail in and a train arrive over the jigsaw of clotheslines and faded, lime-washed roofs. Every prospect was light and naive—like a child's picture book. In the mornings in Sousse I awoke to invigorating salt air, blood oranges, and the smell of mint and rich tobacco wafting from the cafes. The sea was like a panel of blue marble. A few warm, sunny days here made up for the weeks of cold and rain in the interior steppeland.

Geography had defined Sousse's history and atmosphere as it had Kairouan's. Whereas Kairouan was sand, stone, and

Islamic dynasties, Sousse was a pastiche of seafaring civilizations. Agathocles, in the course of his invasion of Carthage, besieged the Phoenician town here in 310 B.C. Hannibal used the city as a military base toward the end of the Second Punic War. And having sided with Rome during the Third Punic War, Hadrumetum—as Sousse was then known—was spared from the destruction that befell Carthage and prospered for centuries, becoming the capital of the southern half of Africa Proconsularis. It remained an important port for Vandals, Byzantines, Arabs, Normans, and Spaniards as late as the sixteenth century.

My recollection of that first trip to Sousse burns about as bright as a candle, half-imagined and thus particularly intense. I remember an archaeological garden inside a fort with towering palms, orange trees, and oleander bushes, where an elderly British lady suddenly exclaimed in a weak voice that Sousse, like Jerusalem, had a "genius loci." The garden was part of a museum filled with Roman and early-Christian mosaics. Their durability, size, and dramatic effect made mosaics the dominant art form of North African antiquity, accounting for the earthiness and sensuality of the period. The mosaic artists, who had learned the technique from Greeks, who, in turn, had brought it from Mesopotamia, were limited in the range of colors of stones available: I saw a feast of reds even as many other tones were missing. Walking through the rooms of the fort, it was hard to believe that faces which were at once so frozen and artificial could also be so passionate. There was a Venus that resembled the Virgin Mary, as Christianity began its rise from the living spirit of paganism. Many conversations I have forgotten, but not the images of Neptune conquering the sea, or of an emperor led by a mangy, chafing tiger. The nineteenth-century critic Walter Pater writes that "all art constantly aspires toward the condition of music." Those images in tesserae conjured up exalted symphonies.

In the 1980s, a decade after that first visit to Sousse, a rash of hotels was built that catered to working-class north Europeans: pensioners shuffled alongside beer-bellied skinheads under *Schnell Imbiss* signs; international pop music blared from pizzerias. Tunisian hustlers on loud motorbikes, flirting with overweight blondes, became a common sight.

◎◎

Thirty miles south of Sousse, I came across a colosseum in the desert almost as big as the one in Rome and better preserved, towering above the small village of El Djem. A century earlier, Gide had arrived in El Djem to gaze upon this monster of a ruin. In *The Immoralist,* his protagonist passes the night in "a filthy room" because there is no decent hotel nearby. There still wasn't. I walked up a wind-blown street toward three tiers of flaming colonnades, nearly eighteen centuries old. A lone figure hidden under a brown caftan swished by on a rusted bicycle. Another man was selling rabbits in wired cages. They were the only people on the street. Inside the colosseum, I walked through galleries of headless marble statues. The muezzin's wail echoed loudly off the stones. I peered into stables and dungeons below the arena where beasts, gladiators, and Christians had awaited their fate. Thysdrus in the third century A.D. was one of the richest towns in Roman Africa, surrounded by gardens and olive groves, and the colosseum offered olive oil merchants the distraction of the games. Ragged Berbers had lined up for hours to get seats on the hot stands. Tunisia was the ancient world's principal supplier of lions, and the spectacles here knew no limits of depravity. Unlike at the Colosseum in Rome, where Fiats now belch black exhaust down the Via dei Fori Imperiali, at El Djem it was the past that seemed so real, and the present so forlorn and temporary.

☙❧

From Sousse we continued south along the coast. Sixty miles from the Libyan border we took a car ferry to the island of Djerba, the fabled land of the Lotus-eaters, from where Odysseus and his companions could not bring themselves to leave.

> So off they went and soon enough
> they mingled among the natives, Lotus-eaters, Lotus-eaters
> who had no notion of killing my companions, not at all,
> they simply gave them the lotus to taste instead. . . .
> Any crewmen who ate the lotus, the honey-sweet fruit,
> lost all desire to send a message back, much less return,
> their only wish to linger there with the Lotus-eaters,
> grazing on lotus, all memory of the journey home
> dissolved forever. . . .

The Tunisian landscape achieved a fine synthesis here: the sea lapping up on dunes, ranks of gnarled olive trees as old as the Roman coins that littered the soil, and hundreds of whitewashed domes. The rocket-shaped minarets were only two or three stories high, yet they seemed to soar as if viewed through a distorting mirror. Houmt Souk, the island's capital, was a windswept masterpiece of sand castle contours. In a country of beaten-silver brooches and bangles, and robes of the richest colors, Djerban women outdid them all, wearing broad-brimmed straw hats over flamboyant robes reminiscent of South American Indians. Djerba was African-*cum*-Arab-*cum*-Greek: sleepy, abstract, sybaritic.

I spent part of an afternoon sunbathing on the pale yellow ramparts of the Bordj el Kebir, overlooking small fishing boats with high stern-posts like those of ancient Carthage that stood moored in the mud. There was not a sound or movement, just a faint hum in my ears. The fort had been built in 1284 by Roger de Loria, the "Admiral of Aragon," who attacked the Moorish kingdom of Tunis as part of a larger plan to conquer Sicily, then in the midst of a popular revolt against the onerous rule of the French Angevins. The revolt, known as the Sicilian Vespers, was so named because it began during the vesper services on Easter Monday, the night of March 30–31, of 1282 in Palermo. It provided an opportunity for Aragon, a wealthy kingdom at the foot of the Pyrenees in northeastern Spain, to wrest control of Sicily from the French.

Roger de Loria, the Aragonese commander, was Italian-born but shared the same foster mother as the Infanta Constance of Aragon, and had been taken to Aragon as a twelve-year-old to grow up at court. With a navy composed of Sicilians and Catalonians, Roger de Loria landed in the middle of the night on Djerba, raided Houmt Souk, and built this fort prior to his attack on Sicily. It was an era when national identity was fluid and world politics a game of aristocratic elites, who often had more in common with each other than with their own peasants at home: it was not unusual for an Italian-born admiral to fight in the service of a Spanish kingdom, while employing sailors from other countries. Lying on the ramparts of Roger's sun-splashed fort filled me with thoughts that, despite the beauty of the island and the spell it cast, made me restless to move on.

∞

We met Abdullah on a bus en route back to Tunis from Djerba. He wore a rumpled suit and had a dark complexion and callused hands. He asked us where we were from, and where we were going. Our answers were perfunctory. He switched from French to English and talked about Sartre and Lamartine. He told us that the Jews of Israel should "be thrown into the sea," adding that he wanted to go to Paris to study philosophy and languages. Then he invited us to his house. When we asked him where he lived, he pointed "out there," across a lonely plateau to a line of terra-cotta hills. The bus stopped at a village with a few cinder block stores where he got off. A few days later, we returned by bus to the same village.

For an hour we walked across the plateau, traversing three wadis. The wind and wild dogs howled in our ears, drowning out the stony solitude. Finally we spotted three mud-walled huts in a valley. Abdullah ran toward us. *"Lehbess!"* he exclaimed, a local Arabic greeting. We hugged like long-lost friends. Of course, we were guilty of self-dramatization, the sin of travelers who try to create poignant memories in advance.

Abdullah introduced us to a succession of people, each of whom hugged us and screamed *Lebbess!* There was his father, Larabi; his mother, Maryam; his grandmother, Hada; his uncle, Chedli; and Abdullah's younger brothers, Kamal, Salem, Rashid, and Moncef. The men had bad teeth, leathery faces, wore ragged caftans, and carried walking sticks. The women were tiny, with faces more leathery than the men's, and adorned with bangles and tattoos like the Zlass women we had seen on the bus from Kairouan to Sousse. Only Abdullah wore western clothes. They were settled nomads, who had lived on the plateau for a generation raising sheep. I remember treeless sunlight, as intense as a search lamp, and constant shouting in my ears: the ceaseless wind had given them the habit of talking loud. Inside the houses, the walls were blackened from woodsmoke. One of the women served us water in whiskey glasses: cold, metallic, delicious. Then came dark, syrupy tea boiled with sugar on a camper stove. Everyone stared at us.

Abdullah's father slaughtered a chicken for the couscous that night. Abdullah proudly displayed his small collection of French and English books, and an old shortwave radio with which he listened to foreign news whenever he could find batteries in the local bazaar. Besides Sartre and Lamartine, he spoke of Frantz Fanon, an anti-colonialist writer from Martinique radicalized by his work as a psychiatrist in the Algerian Civil War, who believed that the peoples of the Third World would bring a new humanism to the planet.

He quoted Fanon's description of America as "a monster, in which the taints, the sickness, and the inhumanity of Europe have grown to appalling dimensions." Abdullah gave me my first real exposure to Third World politics, in which men of humble backgrounds learned about the injustices of their condition from grand ideas that they came across in books. At first I argued, but then I just listened and copied down what he said.

We all slept together on the mud floor. There was no electricity. Breakfast was an oily bowl full of tomato paste and flour into which we dipped pieces of coarse bread. In the morning, I helped Abdullah load up the donkeys with large, empty cans for water at the spring a mile away. On the way we passed a stone olive press that dated from Roman times. A pack of wild dogs approached. Abdullah threw a few stones in their direction and they ran away when one of them was hit. Stones covered the ground everywhere in North Africa and the Middle East, on the steppe and in the desert: unyielding and clarifying, the horrid gray essence of things. People fought over them, they fought with them. It was a landscape that reduced politics to a survival struggle.

That night we had another feast of couscous, and Abdullah's younger brothers recited poems in French for us. In the pre-dawn darkness, Abdullah escorted us back across the freezing, windy plateau to the village, where we sipped tea until the bus came.

The next time I saw Abdullah was seventeen years later when I tracked him down in Tunis, where he was working in a hospital as a male nurse and living in a suburb with a government-subsidized mortgage. We talked about cars and health care. He told me that he wanted to give up smoking. The radicalism was so far in the past he could barely remember it. Tunisia's investment in social welfare had dampened the fires of extremism that engulfed its neighbors. Tunisia was not a democracy. But it was a real state, thanks in part to the legacy of Carthage and Rome.

෨෨

On the way back to Tunis we passed the remains of a massive aqueduct that the Romans had built in Zaghouan to supply water to Carthage fifty miles away. According to legend, a Roman soldier had fallen in love with a native princess, who said she would never marry him until the waters of Zaghouan flowed to Carthage. After the aqueduct was completed, the soldier went to claim his bride, who in despair threw herself from its summit. In *Rome in Africa,* the British scholar Susan Raven writes, "The sheer size of the Roman conception required an imaginative leap which took civil engineering right beyond the dictates of immediate necessity or religious awe. . . . They applied their minds and skills to mastering their environment to an unprecedented degree." The towering procession of moldering stone arches strung across the plain never ceased to amaze me whenever I passed it on my way in or out of Tunis. The smallness and closeness of the mountains made the aqueduct appear larger than it was: the Tunisian landscape was the illustrated history textbook that I had never found in high school or college.

Zaghouan was also the setting for the dramatic conclusion of Flaubert's *Salammbô.* Here a Carthaginian force under Hamilcar trapped the Libyan mercenaries in a narrow pass.

Starving, the mercenaries resorted to cannibalism. When they begged Hamilcar's troops for mercy, the Carthaginians, after binding their arms and legs, crushed them with elephants. "Their chests cracked like boxes being broken. . . ." Others were crucified. "Do you remember the lions crucified on the road to Sicca Veneria?" one dying mercenary said to his comrade on the next cross. "They were our brothers!" the other replied.

Many of the mercenaries went bravely to their deaths. Like soldiers throughout history, they did so not out of patriotism, but out of fear of seeming cowardly in front of their comrades. The final battle of the Mercenary War was fought just beyond Zaghouan in Rhades, now a suburb of Tunis. The Carthaginians had fourteen thousand men, twice that of the mercenaries. Flaubert ends the passage with a description of lions torpidly digesting the corpses.

☙

Before we left Tunisia we visited the ruins of Utica, twenty-five miles north of Tunis and not far from the sea, by the banks of the Oued Medjerda, a partially silted river which flows across northern Tunisia from the mountains of Algeria. The road was lined with eucalyptus trees under a plum-blue sky. The cries of the birds punctuated the silence. Dark cypresses and walnut trees clashed with the orange soil, studded with cyclamens and other mid-winter wildflowers. The maze of scaly Punic and Roman walls, scrubbed and ravaged by time, was covered in vines and moss. A few surviving mosaics lay on the ground: a beadwork of fine, grayish-white pebbles. It was as though the ruins had been placed here deliberately to highlight the natural beauty of the setting. Nearby were haystacks and a Bedouin encampment.

Utica, founded in 1101 B.C., was the oldest Phoenician settlement in what the Romans would later call Africa. Even after Carthage had risen to dominance, Utica remained a vibrant commercial center. It sided with Rome during the Third Punic War, and after Carthage was razed to the ground, Utica enjoyed the rank of *civitas libera,* becoming the principal city in Africa until the Romans completed the rebuilding of Carthage. Here in 46 B.C., Cato the Younger, who led a revolt against Julius Caesar in defense of the democratic ideals of the Roman Republic, committed suicide after he had been surrounded by Caesar's troops. Fighting first in Sicily and then in Albania, Cato had crossed the Mediterranean and marched westward across the Libyan desert. He holed up in Utica in the hope that a republican force would defeat Caesar at Thapsus, a few miles south of Sousse. When he received news of the republican defeat, Cato locked the gates of Utica and evacuated his soldiers by sea before taking his own life with a sword: dying as "the only free and only undefeated man" in Rome, according to Plutarch. At Dyr- rhachium in Albania, writes Plutarch, whereas Pompey had been met with a cold response when he addressed the troops, the Roman soldiers shouted their approval when Cato spoke philosophically about liberty and manly virtue.

Hitchhiking had been difficult that afternoon, and we walked a bit through drowsy fields along the narrow tree- lined road to Tunis. We crossed the Oued Medjerda by foot over a small and handsome Roman bridge: this was before the present highway was built that changed the landscape and removed the Bedouin encampment. I remember looking down at the trickling water and seeing a vision of heaven moving slowly beneath my feet. It seems so long ago, closing the distance with antiquity.

❦5❧

# THE BEAUTY OF GRAY

After midnight on February 11, 1976, I stood on the freezing deck of the S.S. *Calabria,* immersed in the smells of sea and oil, feeling the shudder of metal as the wind rose and we crept out of the harbor. Then the pilot boat turned back and except for the gulls, sliding into new patterns over the deck, the last winking light of La Goulette surrendered to the bobbing horizon and Tunisia dissolved into memory.

The winter sky tingled with stars: a vast monstrance displaying its sacred relics. Orion the Hunter wore his belt of gold, his front foot the star Rigel 545 light-years away. The light I saw that night had left the star during the Hafsid reign in Tunis, when there were men still alive who had discussed philosophy with Ibn Khaldun. Close by were the

Pleiades, the Great Bear, Hyades, and "bright Arcturus," in Virgil's words, describing Aeneas' voyage to Sicily from North Africa. Homer writes about the same winter starscape in the course of Odysseus' departure from Calypso's isle, identified by some as Malta, off Sicily's southern coast.

There could be no two wanderers over these nighttime seas as different from each other as Odysseus and Aeneas. Odysseus suppresses his kingly appetites and trusts the lowliest persons in a desperate struggle to reach home, where only the dreary hardships of domestic life await him. "Many cities of men he saw and learned their minds, many pains he suffered, heartsick. . . ." The *Odyssey* is a poem of war-time survival, of finding one's way back home; whereas the *Aeneid* is a poem about beginning anew because you can't go home again. While Odysseus toils homeward, Aeneas sails westward from his lost Troy to reach Italy and establish the universal civilization that Rome would one day become. In ages of interminable conflict, it is Virgil's *Aeneid* which inspires us with its lofty goals. But in serene ages, it is Homer who more tangibly recalls the vigor and energy of heroic struggle. My interest in these two epic poems grew with each sea crossing that winter: romance is the catalyst of a true education.

The eight-hour journey from the northeast tip of Tunisia to the northwest tip of Sicily provided the illusion of gliding over a map. I sailed from one continent to another over open seas, yet the voyage was short enough that I barely slept. I experienced the progression of the ship eastward, rather than going to bed and waking up in a different place. Nor was there the oceanic turmoil as in that vast and deep stretch between France and Tunisia. The sea was a gently breathing mirror reflecting the starscape. The boat slapped easily over the water, abounding with fish and sponges. I never felt far from the calming embrace of civilization.

I was crossing the old geologic land bridge between Europe and Africa, of which Sicily and other smaller islands like Malta and Pantelleria were the remnants. Tunisia and Sicily were linked by the same mountain chain, whose tallest ridge, underwater for the past 44 million years, divides the Mediterranean into western and eastern halves. Both Islam and Christianity easily forded this strategic channel, eighty miles wide at its narrowest point and the shallowest stretch of the Mediterranean. Sicily had been a Moslem emirate until the French Norman conquest of the eleventh century, even as Christian merchants dominated the souks of Tunisia. Up through the sixteenth century, politicians in Palermo were hatching plans for the conquest of Tunis. A rival of Naples to the north, Palermo derived its power from its economic relationship with North Africa. But modernization hardened the division between Moslem and Christian civilizations. The books that came with the invention of movable type intensified contacts among readers of Arabic and among those of Italian, so that the gulf widened between the two. The Industrial Revolution, moreover, encouraged Italian unification as part of the rise of nation-states, drawing Palermo into the orbit of Naples, Florence, and Rome. By the time of my travels, Tunisia and Sicily were farther apart culturally than ever before in history.

There were only a few passengers on board. I spent part of the night talking with a Nigerian, a man from the Moslem north. He appeared to have no destination. For a decade, he told me, his wanderings had been within the confines of the Sahara: Upper Volta, Niger, Chad, Sudan, Libya, and Tunisia. "How did you manage?" I asked him. "You see, sir, it was easy. I rode local autobuses and stayed at modest-priced hotels." I marveled at his quaint language. He called me "sir," though I was younger and smaller, perhaps because I was white. When he laughed I thought his belly would move the whole ship. We were alone on deck under an emergency *uscita* lamp. He never told me his name or the town he was from. "I've never been to Europe, sir. But I am prepared. I read." He had two books in his large pockets: Plato's *Republic* and *A Concise History of British Common Law.* They were in no better condition than the clothes he wore and the once white towel around his neck. "Where are you headed?" I asked. "I do not know, sir, not exactly. Maybe England to study law." "Do you have friends or relatives there?" "No, sir, but there are many Nigerians in London." He smiled. His innocence awed me. "Where's your pack?" "Well, sir, it's lost. But I am missing only some clothes and a tooth brush." He fit into no category. He was as individual as the night itself, and disappeared with it. I did not see him in the morning when we disembarked. The aura of mystery that surrounded him provided me with a momentary spark of inspiration: *Someday I'll get to the places he talked about.*

The sea emerged from the night an inky silver-blue. Favignana and Levanzo, two off-shore islands, surged out of the water as suggestive as myths: in their smoky unreality they were less like landscapes than reminiscences of them. The oily light of daybreak soon revealed almond trees in lavender bloom. Winds flared. There was a rinsed sharpness to everything, owing to the sudden absence of dust. Europe had arrived, Africa was behind us. On the mainland, the mountain of Érice—tinted red at this hour—soared off the flat plain like a storybook cut-out from Virgil's *Aeneid*. A beacon for sailors, Érice (ancient Eryx) had been the place where Aeneas' father, Anchises, died and where a shrine was built to honor him.

Jetties rose up beside the ship, dividing the sea into smooth rectangles that flashed in the mid-winter sun like painted blue tiles. A sulfur wash seemed to coat the no-longer-distant facades of the port, glassy from a pre-dawn rain. A small building with barricades separated the disembarkation point from a street where people were walking and driving to work. A customs official asked us to open our bags. As soon as we did so, he said *bene* and chalked them. Another official stamped our passports. A few moments later we were within Trápani's cobblestone defiles, looking up at a church with a massive Gothic window and portal. Wrought iron balconies shimmered under street lamps still lit from the previous night. In a small market I saw massive yellow peppers, purplish cabbage, greenish cauliflowers so bright they seemed almost to glow.

We found a cafe bordered by leather and antique shops. In the clutter of liqueurs, richly brewed coffee, and the women in fashionable capes emitting the animal scents of fine perfumes, Tunisia evaporated, its rich sensuality appearing austere against the new surroundings. After the spare geometries of North Africa, the umber baroque buildings seemed to welcome us in a warm embrace.

Fine distinctions and relativities are the essence of travel, for comparison is the basis of sound analysis. Later, when I would journey to northern Italy, the distinctions between Sicily and Tunisia would fade somewhat. But I was never so alert as to what marked off North Africa from Europe as I was those first moments in Trápani. That morning I resolved to take notes upon every new arrival. It was the drama of such arrivals that encouraged my self-confidence, even as my résumé was blank: ever-shifting scenery provides the illusion of endless opportunities.

Watching the men and women gathering at the polished counter for their espresso and *cornetti,* I saw how much more urbane and relaxed with each other they were than the young men and women of Tunisia. Sexual rhythms here were more liquid, less ritualized: in Tunisia, the women were like distant, costumed statuary, while young men gathered in village cafes, the dirt caked under their fingernails, smoldering in boredom. Despite the traditions and refinements that had so captured me—owing to the settlement pattern bequeathed by the Romans—Tunisia, from the vantage point of Sicily, appeared less stable than I had earlier thought: more likely to be undermined by some future unrest.

Of course, Trápani (Punic *Drepanon,* meaning "sickle"), with its bister hills and black shadows, was practically a marchland of North Africa. This city was three thousand years old, settled by the Phoenicians as part of the expansion of their new western empire, anchored by Carthage and Utica. It was in Trápani—Carthage's principal naval station for the defense of Sicily—that the Roman fleet had been defeated in 250 B.C. during the First Punic War. (Though the Romans scored a decisive victory nine years later off Favignana and Levanzo.) The Arabs have a long tradition here: couscous is a culinary staple and Trápani's old city is a legacy of the medieval Arab town.

Trápani's position, guarding the channel that divides Europe from Africa, made for a rich history in which to plunge. Travel offers the best kind of loneliness, since real adventure is not about physical risk but about the acquisition of knowledge. The war stories told by foreign correspondents around bar tables get stale, but the stories that age slower, but which are harder to communicate, are those regarding a thought or perception that may have been kindled by a mere line of text, or shard of stone.

❦

My next vivid memory of that first day in Sicily came in the late afternoon: a visit to the Pepoli National Museum, whose mustard-yellow cloister was punctuated by palms, oleanders, and Punic ruins. A Gothic portico led to a grand staircase inlaid with geometric Arab mosaics. At the top were halls of Greek amphorae, Byzantine icons, Islamic tapestries, and early modern paintings. It was my introduction to Sicily's civilizational transformations.

Sicily, the largest island in the Mediterranean, is the breakwater between the sea's eastern and western halves. It is the meeting ground not only of Europe and Africa, but of the Greek and Latin worlds. Every great Mediterranean civilization occupied Sicily and left its footprint: Phoenician, Greek, Roman, Arab; as well as Vandal, Byzantine, and a host of North European ones, particularly that of the French Normans. The word "mafia" may be derived from the Arabic *mahjas,* for "boasting." Organized crime in Sicily is a manifestation of millennia of occupation that, except for a few golden ages, inflicted poverty, stifled the development of institutions and national consciousness, and called for informal means of protection against the threat of even worse anarchy.

According to the Greeks, the history of Sicily begins with the one-eyed Cyclopes: the very personification of anarchy. Homer describes the Cyclopes in the *Odyssey* as "high and mighty . . . lawless brutes" who never plant or till the soil since "the earth teems with all they need."

> They have no meeting place for council, no laws either,
> no, up on the mountain peaks they live in arching caverns—
> each a law to himself, ruling his wives and children,
> not a care in the world for any neighbor.

Myths offer ultimate, condensed truth: so much more useful for our understanding than the tedium of mere facts. The image of the Cyclopes is visual shorthand for how the earliest Greek travelers saw the indigenous inhabitants of Italy and Sicily, who had no laws and, therefore, no civilization. Following the Cyclopes, the cannibalistic Laestrygones, the aboriginal Sicanians of western Sicily, and the enigmatic Elymians (descendants of the Trojans who sailed here from fallen Troy) came the Sicels, from whom Sicily gets its name. The Sicels spoke a language akin to Latin. They migrated into the eastern part of Sicily from mainland Italy around 1250 B.C. Because of Sicily's sheer size and rugged terrain, different parts of the island could be occupied by different peoples scarcely aware of each other's existence. The Phoenicians built settlements on the western coast at the same time that they were settling Carthage, and soon afterwards the Greeks settled the eastern coast, overrunning the Sicels. The Greeks introduced the culture of the vine and the olive to Sicily, ending the Neolithic phase of the island's history and beginning the Mediterranean one. (Later, the Arabs would help introduce the lemon to Sicily and the Portuguese the orange.)

As the Phoenician and Greek civilizations matured and spread throughout the island, conflicts arose both among the Greeks themselves and between the Greeks and the Phoenicians that led to military interventions by mainland Greece, Carthage, and Rome. The Athenians invaded in the late fifth century B.C., and the Punic Wars broke out here in the third century B.C. Thus was Sicily sucked into the whirlpool of Mediterranean history.

Given its geographical centrality, it may be only an accident that Sicily ended up in modern times as an exotic backwater rather than a political giant. In the middle of the seventh century A.D., Byzantine emperor Constans II moved his capital from Constantinople to Syracuse on Sicily's southeastern coast, to protect his empire from Arab invaders. Had his tyrannical behavior not inspired his chamberlain to assassinate him in his bathtub on September 15, 668, the Byzantine capital might have remained in Sicily, and the subsequent history of the Mediterranean might have been quite different.

๑๑

Winter in Sicily back then was a time of rolled-up awnings, half-empty hotels, and lonely, unkempt archaeological sites, allowing you to imagine an even earlier age of travel. We slept late the following morning, then took the bus from Trápani to Érice. As the bus mounted the switchbacks, the islands of Favignana and Levanzo loomed like planets in the heavens as the sea, far below us now, assumed the dimensions and consistency of the sky. I saw a terrain of bleak limestone stubbled with pine brush: elephant tusks have been found in caves on the mountainside here, proof of Sicily's African origins. Only 2,454 feet at the summit, Érice seems higher because of the sharp drop in temperature and its isolation, without another mountain or hill nearby.

Then, just as we alighted from the bus, came a bosky realm of spiny cypresses and birches guarding a village of red roof tiles, bleached to pale ivory and blackened with moss. Wet flagstone alleys leaned into the sky, or curved into the obscurity of a dimly lit painting. Érice was a scape of ruins wrapped in a thick mist that was forever being rent, revealing this or that Gothic portal: San Martino, for instance, once a dull red and now a watery, smoke-blackened pink. The Norman and Gothic facades had been reduced by centuries of wind and rain. It was a place of whispers: the spiritual heart of the sun-drenched Mediterranean imprisoned in a cold, monastic darkness.

Érice is named for Eryx, the son of Aphrodite, a local king who hosted Herakles when he visited Sicily. It was settled first by the Elymians, who came from Anatolia and survived here through their ability to assimilate other cultures: Phoenician, Greek, and finally Roman. The fertility cult that arose at Érice worshiped the Phoenician Astarte, reborn as the Greek Aphrodite and the Roman Venus, whose temple the emperor Claudius lavishly restored in the middle of the first century A.D. In the spring, doves were released from Érice toward a sister fertility shrine at Sicca Veneria across the sea in Tunisia. In the Middle Ages the Arabs built a fortress here, which the French Norman count Roger I attacked in 1077. The present village dates from the Norman Conquest.

The gray of Érice's cobbles and flagstones evoked depth and introspection, erasing the exhilarating spell of Trápani's early morning pigments. Like water at dusk, gray is the elemental color, holding the memory of everything that human beings have experienced. The gray of Érice was a pull toward maturity, a return to Rodin's garden.

Descending the curved, gray staircase in Érice's civic museum, staring at a bust by the window, I said to myself, *I'll remember this day, this staircase.* That moment I was comfortable and content, full of plans and inspiration built on insecurity. But I didn't remember the moment quite correctly, it turns out. When I returned to the museum twenty-five years later, the gray stone staircase was there all right. But it wasn't curved. And there was no bust. There was a Punic jar that—seeing it again after so many years—I suddenly recalled. *Of course. It was a jar, not a bust!* I recalled, too, albeit vaguely, a medieval wooden panel hanging on the wall. What I had no memory of was a lavish fragment of blue and orange tile on the ledge beside the Punic jar—in Arab-Byzantine style, inscribed with the word "PAX." But it had always been there, a museum guard told me.

Looking at the piece of tile made me remember a fleeting idea that I had barely nurtured and long forgotten. It had induced me to want to remember the moment in the first place: *Such interesting objects,* I had told myself, *each separated from the other by centuries, could be connected only through a lifetime of study, and what would be a better way to spend a lifetime?* That idea had put me on a trail of knowledge and experiences, the weight of which submerged the momentary insight that started it all, as well as the memory of the objects associated with it.

On my return visit I also sought out the little library that I had passed through at the top of the stairs, with its old card catalogues and melancholy bindings, in order to reach a small collection of Punic, Egyptian, and Hellenistic objects. The librarians turned their heads up at me as I disturbed their domain, just as a previous generation of librarians had done long ago, releasing another flow of recollection.

We cannot be completely happy in the present because we must be conscious of all the tedium and worries accompanying it. It is only the moments that are free of such tedium that constitute real happiness: like that moment on the museum staircase a quarter century before. But such a moment is composed of so many extraordinary and distinct elements, the memory of which vanishes within hours, or minutes. To recall unawares a few of those elements is, according to Beckett, like breathing "the true air of Paradise."

≈6≈

# THE SPEECHLESS TEMPLE

We interrupted the three-hour train trip from Trápani to Palermo with a stop at Segesta, the site of a Greek Doric temple from the fifth century B.C. The sleepy, dusty station had a left-luggage office where we deposited our bags so that we could hike to the temple, a mile away. The countryside was a gentle roller coaster of dipping valleys and massive hills: a bright green and yellow tartan of olive and wheat fields, creased by rushing ravines and with myrtles and agave cactuses. As we walked we heard the tinkle of goat bells. The Greek temple loomed in the distance, a gray and speechless bearer of secrets. Bernard Berenson, the Renaissance art critic who made his home in Italy, calls it "an affirmation of reason, order and intelligence in the midst of the pell-mell, the indifference and the anarchy of nature." Goethe wrote about how the "wind howled around the columns as though they were a forest. . . ." When I took that walk I had never heard of Berenson and knew nothing about Goethe's visit. It was the unforgettable memory of that temple in the middle of an overgrown field that led me to them.

We tiptoed around the columns, ducking in and out of loud, fresh breezes. There was no one else there, and little sign of habitation for miles. Wildflowers littered the February fields. The Greek temple, begun in 430 B.C. at the time of Segesta's alliance with Athens, was never completed because of a war that erupted between Segesta and the city-state of Selinunte to the south. It was a quarrel that set off a chain of events leading Athens to invade Sicily. There was no roof, the columns had been left unfluted, and the abacuses were rough. The lack of finish only added to the temple's brawn and monumentality.

From the temple we hiked another mile to a Greek theater that offered a panoramic prospect of the nearby mountains. The roar of the wind intensified the silence. We arrived tired and thirsty back at the desolate train station, where we finished a half liter of wine and a large bowl of tomato pasta with basil. It was served by an old woman who, when we asked for the bill, told us to pay whatever we thought was a fair amount.

That brief stop at Segesta—lasting but a few hours—drew me to my first encounter with Thucydides' *Peloponnesian War,* as well as other books that examined the ill-fated Athenian invasion of Sicily. Associated as it was in my mind with a lovely landscape and a perfect afternoon, I felt from the outset that it was history worth knowing.

❦

The story begins in 427 B.C., when the Athenians sent twenty ships to southeastern Sicily, where their allies from the city-state of Leontini were threatened by a group of adjacent city-states, dominated by Syracuse. Syracuse was sympathetic to Sparta, which was locked in a bipolar conflict with Athens for control of the Greek archipelago: the Peloponnesian War.

Two years later, the Athenians sent forty more ships to assist their allies in Sicily, believing that with the additional application of force, the war would soon end. But that same summer, the Syracusans occupied Messina, in northeastern Sicily, at the invitation of the Greek inhabitants. Fighting consequently erupted between Athenians, Leontines, and indigenous Sicels on one side, and Syracusans and Messinians on the other. Athens' hesitant intervention had only brought it the hatred of many more Greeks in Sicily.

At a gathering in the southern coastal town of Gela in 424 B.C., the Syracusan nobleman Hermocrates argued for peace among the Greek cities of Sicily, so that they could more effectively confront Athens. His speech is recorded by Thucydides:

> Vengeance is not necessarily successful because wrong has been done, or strength sure because it is confident; but the incalculable element in the future exercises the widest influence, and is the most treacherous, and yet in fact the most useful of things, as it frightens us all equally, and thus makes us consider before attacking each other.

A more eloquent plea for caution in foreign policy has rarely been uttered; nor has such cool philosophy ever been improved upon. The shrewdness of the ancients, unclouded by sentimentality, is mirrored in the confident tranquility of their statuary. Hermocrates succeeded in his plea and the city-states of Sicily united against the common enemy. The Athenians, bereft momentarily of local allies, sailed home.

But that is only the prologue to the tragedy that would soon unfold:

In 416 B.C., envoys from Segesta arrived in Athens with an urgent request. The Segestans had gone to war with their neighbors the Selinuntines over a disputed border. The Selinuntines had the help of their allies, the Syracusans, and now the Segestans were reminding the Athenians of their mutual alliance, which had led to the construction of the temple. The Segestans told the Athenians that if Syracuse wasn't stopped, it would conquer eventually the whole of Sicily, and would then join forces with Sparta to topple Athens. Fearing a domino effect, the Athenians sent envoys to Segesta to reassess their ally's wealth and strength.

The people of Segesta were Elymians who had adopted Greek culture (unlike the Elymians of Érice, who had adopted Punic culture). However, the Segestans were quite poor. In order to deceive the Athenian envoys about their wealth and power, the Segestans borrowed gold and silver drinking cups from their wealthier Elymian cousins in Érice, and flaunted them in the houses where the Athenians had been invited to stay. It is possible that work on the temple was begun or accelerated at this time to impress the Athenians, who went home with exaggerated notions of their ally's resources. And so, in 415 B.C., the Athenians voted to send sixty ships to help Segesta against Selinunte. The fleet would be under the command of Alcibiades, Nicias, and Lamachus. The first two, Alcibiades and Nicias, are among the most intriguing figures in classical history.

Alcibiades, thirty-five years old at the time of the Sicilian Expedition, was vain, handsome, ostentatious, the heir to great wealth by marriage, and a notorious paramour. He was also brave, operationally brilliant, and blessed with a keen instinct about men that allowed him to manipulate his allies and take advantage of his adversaries. He was the kind of diplomat, general, or politician who was full of savvy, intimidating bombast, and charisma, a combination that made him as effective as he was insufferable; yet he lacked a certain tragic sensibility, otherwise known as wisdom, which might have restrained his appetite for costly overseas adventures.

According to Plutarch, Alcibiades oozed ambition. He was a media star before the term was invented. He lost his father at a young age and became the ward and protégé of the great Athenian statesman Pericles. Deprived of fatherly oversight even as he was exposed to brilliant teachers such as Socrates, Alcibiades became sophisticated in argument while often unwise in his decisions. A dove at first on the subject of Sparta, he suddenly became a hawk when it came to intervention in Sicily. Speaking before the Athenian assembly upon return of the envoys from Segesta, Alcibiades argued that as a great power, Athens had a responsibility to its allies which if shirked would threaten the values Athenians held dear. Alcibiades saw Athens' empire as virtually illimitable: "We cannot fix the exact point at which our empire shall stop," he said with his quickness for rhetoric, "we have reached a position in which we must not be content with retaining what we have but must scheme to extend it for, if we cease to rule others, we shall be in danger of being ruled ourselves." He argued further that the Greek city-states of Sicily were "peopled by motley rabbles," that they had weak institutions, lacked patriotism as the Athenians with their democracy defined it, and could thus easily be defeated. It was a speech in which arrogance was combined with wishful thinking.

Countering Alcibiades was Nicias, a man of excessive caution, twenty years older, who had invested his wealth in silver mines. Nicias had several minor military victories to his credit and six years earlier, in 421 B.C., he had negotiated a detente with Sparta that historians refer to as the Peace of Nicias: a peace which Alcibiades was now determined to undermine, making the two men mortal enemies.

Nicias told the assembly that while he would share command of the expedition with Alcibiades and Lamachus, he could not recommend it. Athens, he said, should not be "grasping at another empire before we have secured the one we have already." The truce that he had negotiated with Sparta was still precarious, he warned. Rebels in Chalcidice in northern Greece had yet to be subdued. "I affirm, then, that you leave many enemies behind you here to go there far away and bring back more with you." In any case, he continued, Sicily was too far away to be permanently suppressed. Even if the Greek cities in Sicily united under Syracuse, they would be unlikely to attack Athens, and Athens' reputation for power in Sicily would be the higher for being untested.

"Our struggle, therefore, if we are wise, will not be for the barbarian Segestans, but to defend ourselves most effectively against the oligarchic machinations of Sparta."

In contrast to Alcibiades, Nicias described the Hellenic cities of Sicily as stable and formidable: not even the Carthaginians could subdue them. Nor should the Segestans be trusted, he said, since it was in their interest "to lie as well as they can. . . ." Because of Sicily's strength and great distance from Athens, he warned that only an expedition with forces drawn from throughout the empire would succeed.

But Nicias' speech backfired. Rather than quell the ardor of the interventionists, it stoked their enthusiasm further. The Athenian assembly, heeding his advice, dispatched one hundred triremes to Sicily, in addition to transport ships and five thousand hoplites, or heavily armed infantrymen. From a small incursion of twenty ships a decade earlier, Athens had been lured by its allies deeper into the affairs of Sicily, so that now, because of the miscalculation of its most cautious of statesmen, the prestige of Athens' entire maritime empire was dependent upon a military victory in that distant land.

As I became acquainted with this history, it was impossible for me not to think of President Lyndon Johnson dispatching half a million American troops to South Vietnam a decade after President Dwight Eisenhower had sent a small amount of military aid there. The differences between the Athenian misadventure in Sicily and America's in Vietnam—which came to an inglorious end six months before I set out for the Mediterranean—seemed less interesting than the similarities.

The Athenian expedition ran almost immediately into difficulties. Arriving off Sicily's coast, the Athenians were told that the Segestans could afford only thirty talents for their own defense. Nicias, unsurprised at the news, advised that the Athenians sail their armada past Selinunte and other pro-Syracusan cities, in an attempt to coerce them into a settlement with Segesta, and then sail home. But Alcibiades demanded that Syracuse be attacked. So the Athenians sailed to Catánia, north of Syracuse, and forced their way into the city and used it as a base from which to attack Syracusan territory. Complicating matters was the city-state of Camarina, a Cambodian-style neutral that sympathized with Athens, but feared Syracuse more, because it was nearby. Thus, it opted for positive neutrality in favor of the Syracusans.

Athenians, meanwhile, were being swept up in a series of domestic protests related to the mutilation of the Hermae—square pillars supporting busts of the god Hermes with male genitals, which stood as guardians at the crossroads of Greek cities. Alcibiades, whose unrestrained ambition had attracted many enemies, was accused of complicity in their mutilation, and he was summoned home from the expedition to face trial. The heated political atmosphere inspired a new fear among Athenians that a tyranny would be reestablished. Criticism of their own democracy became so intense in Athens that some even expressed sympathy for their arch-enemy Sparta.

Rather than return to an uncertain future in Athens, Alcibiades escaped to Sparta. The Athenians then condemned him to death in absentia. But Alcibiades was resourceful. He convinced the Spartans to dispatch a force to Syracuse to help it defeat Nicias. While he could respect the Spartans for fighting their foes, he told them, he could not respect his enemies at home in Athens who had robbed his beloved land of its honor. When the Spartans tired of him, Alcibiades crossed over to the Persian commander Tissaphernes, and persuaded him to play Athens and Sparta off against each other.

Soon afterwards, Alcibiades was helped by allies in Samos to take command of Athenian ships in the Hellespont, and in a series of naval engagements he recovered Chalcidice and Byzantium from Sparta in 410 B.C. The victories allowed him to return to Athens as a hero, and the previous charges against him were dropped. But after military setbacks elsewhere, he switched sides again—now to the Persian general Pharnabazus, a rival of Tissaphernes. It was in Pharnabazus' camp in Asia Minor, in 404 B.C., that Alcibiades was assassinated in a joint Spartan-Persian plot. The French historian Marguerite Yourcenar, in her fictionalized memoir of the Roman emperor Hadrian, suggests that "Alcibiades had seduced everyone and everything, even History herself; and nevertheless he left behind him mounds of Athenian dead, abandoned in the quarries of Syracuse, his own country on verge of collapse, and the gods of the crossroads drunkenly mutilated by his hands."

His treachery and hypocrisy notwithstanding, had Alcibiades been allowed to remain part of the joint command in Sicily, his remarkable ability to act in contingencies might have saved the expedition from the disaster that awaited it, especially as Syracuse would not have been bolstered by the Spartan reinforcements inspired by his perfidy.

Once Alcibiades left Sicily and escaped to Sparta, Nicias counseled his men that they were "far from home" without friends, and that the locals would fight desperately for their land. The Athenians would have to be ruthless in order to survive: the enthusiasm with which the Sicilian intervention had begun was thus turned in upon itself.

The Athenians proceeded to triumph in a series of land engagements to Syracuse's rear, but Lamachus was killed, leaving Nicias the sole commander. Just as Nicias was preparing a decisive assault, the Spartans arrived to help the Syracusans. With the tide of battle turning against Athens in 414 B.C., Nicias sent a message home, in which he said that he had either to be reinforced or to pull out. All of Sicily, with the exception of the city-state of Agrigento, was now actively supporting Syracuse. Under fierce attack in the summer of 413 B.C., the Athenians fled to a harbor that they had fortified less than a mile south of Syracuse. Fighting raged. Nicias' troops suffered heavy losses, despite being reinforced by Demosthenes, a highly regarded Athenian general.

Demosthenes called for an immediate withdrawal though Athens had the naval advantage. But Nicias, in a sudden change of heart, overruled him, arguing that while his soldiers proclaimed the danger of their exposed position, once they reached the safety of Athens, they "would proclaim just as loudly the opposite," and their generals would be condemned for cowardice. Having advised originally against the expedition, and having taken command with deep misgiving, Nicias refused, for honor's sake, a precipitous withdrawal. Only when the Spartan commander Gylippus returned with more reinforcements did Nicias finally relent.

The Athenian commanders now secretly planned their

withdrawal even as their troops continued to fight. As casualties mounted, the Athenians despaired: nothing in their great history had prepared them for such a humiliating defeat, or for such a resourceful foe.

The Syracusans trapped the Athenians in the harbor by anchoring triremes and lashing them together with iron chains. With 110 triremes of their own, the decks filled with bowmen and javelin throwers, the Athenians planned to break out and sail to Catánia. They equipped their triremes with grappling hooks to seize hold of the Syracusan ships after ramming them. But the Syracusans countered by throwing slippery hides over their prows. Nicias went from ship to ship, personally addressing the men by name, telling them that their homeland was the freest in the world, and that defeat would lead to the conquest of Athens by Sparta and Syracuse. With two hundred ships ramming each other in a small harbor, it was among the fiercest naval battles in history.

In the end, the Syracusans triumphed. The Athenians abandoned their ships, and made for the shore and then to camp. Panicking, forty thousand Athenian troops and noncombatants made a forced march inland, hoping to link up with friendly Sicels, and leaving behind their sick and wounded, and unburied dead: "Each man as he recognized a friend among them shuddered with grief and horror," writes Thucydides.

Syracusan cavalry and infantry harassed them along the way. Their situation deteriorating, the Athenians secretly left their camp at night and marched back toward the coast. But Demosthenes' force was captured and butchered—only six thousand of his twenty thousand men survived the assault. Nicias' army continued to the Assinarus River, fifteen miles south of Syracuse. There the Syracusans ambushed and massacred the Athenians as they wallowed in the foul and bloody water, dying of thirst.

Gylippus, the Spartan general, wanted to bring Nicias and Demosthenes back in chains to Sparta, but the Syracusans under his command protested and executed the two Athenian generals. Of Nicias, Thucydides writes: "This or the like was the cause of the death of a man who, of all the Hellenes in my time, least deserved such a fate, seeing that the whole course of his life had been regulated with strict attention to virtue."

Whereas Alcibiades was more gifted of instinct and calculation, Nicias may have had the wiser historical sensibility, intuiting from the start that the conquest of Sicily was too grand a conception for even the world's most exceptional power. Yet, while Alcibiades in his treasonous escapades simply ran out of luck, Nicias had little to start with. Indeed, he ended up, in Plutarch's words, suffering "the calamity which he had often predicted." Thus, it is Alcibiades who allures us through the chasm of the millennia with his mercurial behavior and magnetic personality, though Nicias may have been the more substantial, the more complex, and the more honorable figure, a man who, though a poor general, was counted among the greatest citizens of Athens by Aristotle.

The six thousand Athenian survivors labored in the rock quarries of Syracuse before being sold into slavery. Fourteen years had elapsed from Athens' first foray into Sicily to its final disaster there: the same number of years between the early forays of the Kennedy administration and President Ford's final withdrawal from Vietnam. The war split the home front in Athens. Paralyzed by pessimism and recriminations, it was some time before Athenians were willing to resume in earnest the bipolar conflict with Sparta. Sicily, as it turned out, had not been crucial to the survival of Athens' democracy and its maritime empire. For despite having lost and suffered so much, Athens still had the resources to lead an alliance.

Sicily's heritage suggested that Vietnam was less unique than many of my generation supposed. The manifold similarities between the two debacles provided a sense of distance from the latter one. Sicily nurtured my compassion for the American commanders in Vietnam and the civilian officials who prosecuted the war. None was a traitor like Alcibiades, but quite a few were tragic and imperfect in their judgment, like Nicias.

∞

As for the Segestans, surrounded though they were by hostile neighbors, they continued to turn the great powers to their advantage. In 409 B.C., threatened again by Selinunte and with the Athenians gone, Segesta made an alliance with Carthage. But after the First Punic War broke out, Segesta became the first city in Sicily to desert Carthage and link itself with Rome. It did so by killing the Carthaginian garrison that had been stationed in Segesta to protect the inhabitants. Through such deceit Segesta was able to survive until the arrival of Moslem armies in the early Middle Ages.

# A City in Terra-Cotta

Tired and slightly drunk after the hike to the temple and the wine at the railway station, I drifted in and out of sleep on the eastbound train, catching glimpses of soaring, rust-colored massifs that shielded the Tyrrhenian Sea. I awoke before sunset as the train pulled into Palermo.

Palermo assaulted my senses at once. It was a city in terra-cotta, lit by a dying winter sun and teeming with loud children: a more prosperous version of Calcutta, I would later find out, whose hot colors were in various phases of decomposition. Leaving our bags at a cheap pension, we wandered through tenements and winding bazaars that were strung over with ribbons of drying clothes and smelled of fish, spoiled fruit, and fresh flowers. It was shortly before the Lenten carnival and a myriad of baubles overflowed from battered carts. Blood oranges were everywhere. There were so many collapsed roofs that parts of Palermo resembled the tumbledown Kasbah of Algiers, without the sterilizing effects of a crazed socialism followed by an equally crazed Islamism. The faces in the street were full of joy, sadness, and longing; it was as if emotion were an end in itself, with beauty its only purpose. Palermo, brimming with humanity, appeared the opposite of loneliness.

After dark, we paused, exhausted, in a back pew of the Church of Gesù, a sixteenth-century edifice whose crispated, black and white porphyry interior, embellished with gold leaf, manifested a self-assured grandeur. It was artistic elaboration expressing the life force. The first principle of the Sicilian baroque, writes Vincent Cronin in his 1954 book, *The Golden Honeycomb,* "is that nothing shall remain simple: the straight line of a column must be twisted, or the flutings painted." The temple at Segesta was still in my mind, even as I was bewildered by this church.

The next morning organ music and church bells filtered into the courtyard of the regional archaeological museum, where a clay fountain, filled with jungly plants, was encircled by palms, cacti, and banana trees. The statues, like the walls, were the rusty orange of glowing coals. In adjoining rooms Roman torsos and round, sensuous Punic faces sat between cabinets of Greek pottery. The dust gave the place a dreamy aura. Here as elsewhere in Sicily and Tunisia, the sheer quantity of the antiquities, and their organic link to the setting, make the study of them irresistible.

Nearby, we found an Arab-Norman church built in 1143—later given the name of La Martorana, after the founder of a Benedictine order. The baroque interior ran with dark reds and browns, and was illuminated by Byzantine gold pageantry. The fusion of Latin and Greek Christianity—absent from our own age because of the walls of distrust erected by religious schisms, and aggravated by the stresses of modernization—flourished in unison in this as in so many other Sicilian churches. So often in Sicily I would hear Latin melodies against the golden backdrop of Byzantium, beneath the woodwork of Islam, itself influenced by Greece and Rome. Sicily demonstrated that the Mediterranean's most profound impact upon humanity has been the advancement of art and culture through one civilization meeting another. It was in La Martorana that I encountered the medieval personage most responsible for Sicily's cultural eclecticism, in a mosaic on the southern wall: a French Norman king in Byzantine robes under Greek lettering that proclaims a Latin title, *Rogerios Rex.*

❧❧

The most radiant period of Sicilian history (and perhaps of the whole Middle Ages) owes its origin to the inclinations of two brothers from Hauteville, a village near Saint-Lô in rain-lashed Normandy. By the early eleventh century, the Normans had completed a cultural transformation that began a century earlier, in 911, when their Viking forebears sailed up the Seine after crossing the North Sea. By 950, most had been baptized and were speaking French, with Norse used only by the new immigrants living along the coast. Adventurous and energetic, the Normans were natural wanderers and by the early eleventh century the malarial marchlands of southern Italy—contested by the Pope, the Germans, and the Byzantine Greeks—beckoned with opportunities for young Norman soldiers. A grand guignol of sieges and rebellions in the second half of the eleventh century led to the emergence of the Norman Robert of Hauteville as the duke of Apulia and Calabria, even as his brother Roger began his conquest of Sicily.

The emirate of Palermo, at this time, boasting of three hundred mosques, was a cultural and economic hub of the Moslem world, endowed with fountains, gardens, and souks; yet it was weakened by conflicts with the Moslem emirates of Trápani to the west, Agrigento to the south, and Syracuse-Catánia to the southeast, all of which had recently extricated themselves from the domination of the Zirid caliph of Kairouan in Tunisia. On January 5, 1072, Roger's cavalry attacked the Friday Mosque of Palermo and subdued the city after several days of street fighting. But Sicily's rugged topography, with its many hilltop strongholds, helped the Arabs endure, and battles raged for an entire generation: Moslem Sicily would not be conquered until 1094.

The First Crusade was launched the following year. The Christian reconquest of southern Spain still lay centuries ahead. Thus, the bloody and drawn-out Norman takeover of Sicily marks the beginning of the Moslem decline in the Mediterranean, which began to reverse itself only in the second half of the twentieth century with the migration of North African laborers to Europe.

The historian John Julius Norwich writes that at a time of feudal anarchy throughout Europe, when a combination of cynical self-interest and "woolly-headed" religious idealism culminated in the disgrace of the First Crusade, Roger of Hauteville built a strong Sicilian state in which Normans, Latins, Greeks, and Arabs could prosper and get along. He appointed a Greek the "Emir of Palermo," and gave Arabs command of the treasury and of special units in the army. The mosques remained crowded while Christian churches and monasteries rose up around the city. But it was Roger's son, Roger II, who would carry this achievement to unforeseen heights, making medieval Sicily a multicultural model for the early twenty-first century. As globalization dissolved borders in the late 1990s, and cultural and religious tensions rose, I reflected on Norwich's enchanting study of Roger II in twelfth-century Sicily, *The Kingdom in the Sun,* as well as on his earlier work about the Normans, *The Other Conquest,* both of which I first came across as an outcome of my travels in the 1970s.

The universal civilization that is the vision of Virgil's *Aeneid*—a supranational political and spiritual world order—was never closer to fruition than in Sicily under this French Norman king. Roger II of Hauteville, crowned King of Sicily in Palermo on Christmas Day, 1130, thirty-six years after his father had consolidated control over the island, would apply absolutism toward liberal ends: five hundred years before Thomas Hobbes would recommend the same in his *Leviathan.* Of all medieval European monarchs, Roger II may be the most attractive to modern sensibilities. He grew up speaking Latin, Greek, and Arabic as well as French in his father's cosmopolitan court. He combined a gift for diplomacy with an un-Norman-like aversion to war, at which he was, nevertheless, proficient. Because of his diplomatic skills, the Mediterranean world adapted more easily to Sicily's new political and military influence: no insignificant benefit given that the rise of a new power usually stirs international conflict. Nor was Roger II cursed by the religious fatalism common to his time, for which Machiavelli's secular philosophy would later provide the remedy. Whenever Roger II was cornered by adversaries—with his life and throne in danger—rather than slip into depression and mysticism, he always discovered new stores of energy. It was his combination of diplomacy, military know-how (all the more skillful because used sparely), and sheer drive that allowed him to retake the southern Italian mainland after it had slipped back into anarchy, a conquest that would give Sicily the security required for its own economic development.

Roger II was a strategic genius. In 1146 he captured Tripoli in Libya, giving him mastery of North Africa and cutting the Mediterranean in half, so that the ships of the Second Crusade could not sail from the western to the eastern Mediterranean without his consent. Though he gave his official blessing to the Second Crusade, unofficially he frowned on it, just as his father had frowned on the First Crusade: the Norman kingdom of Sicily was built on tolerance and Moslems were among its principal advisors. While the Franks and Byzantines weakened themselves in the Holy Land, Roger II occupied parts of mainland Greece, thereby preventing the Byzantines from threatening southern Italy. For good measure, he backed an insurrection in Serbia through his friends in Hungary that further weakened Byzantium. As a result, by the end of the Second Crusade, Roger II had risen to the rank of the most influential ruler in Europe.

Roger II went far toward solving the foremost philo-
sophical problem of the Middle Ages: that of secular power.
The era was defined, in part, by a vast and ineffectual papal
universality, under which weak and shadowy kingdoms,
duchies, and baronies wallowed in inconclusive wars. But in
twelfth-century Sicily, Roger II ruled absolutely in a style of
oriental magnificence which he borrowed from the Byzantine court in Constantinople, then the only city in Europe
with a larger population than Palermo. The coin that he
introduced, the ducat, showed not the papal symbol of St.
Peter, but Christ Pantocrator ("Lord of the Universe").

And because the Pope had little power in Sicily, Roger
II's political enemies had few means of appeal. The power of
the knights was limited and the strong state built by his
father flourished. It was based largely on Arab and ancient
Roman institutions, and provided the safety and predictabil-
ity which allowed various religious communities to live
without fear of each other, or of the next day.

Roger II's kingdom, which in coastal North Africa
stretched from Algeria to Libya, approximated the contours
of Genseric's Vandal kingdom of seven centuries earlier. His
achievement was great precisely because his hold was so tenuous. Had the Almohad Berbers set out from the Atlas
Mountains in Morocco and conquered Tunisia a few years
earlier than they did, and then gone on to challenge Norman
Sicily, the loyalty of Roger II's Arab subjects could not have
been assured. Indeed, this "baptized sultan" of Sicily ruled a
melange of sectarian communities that constituted a mini-
Byzantine or Ottoman Empire rather than a modern state.
The proficient bureaucratic apparatus girded by a solid na-

tional identity that Cardinal Richelieu would forge in France in the seventeenth century, by challenging both the Pope and the Holy Roman Emperor, was still beyond Roger's grasp. Though, had he lived beyond his fifty-eight years, Roger might have achieved that too.

The churches we visited in Palermo were the mystical accompaniment of Roger's absolute secular power: a power which, by providing a breathing space against the surrounding chaos, unleashed a torrent of liberal learning. In an age when Arabic was an international language of science, Roger's court was dominated by Arab doctors, geographers, and mathematicians. He commissioned the greatest geographical compendium of the Middle Ages, written by his friend, the scholar Abu Abdullah Mohammed al-Edrissi. *The Book of Roger,* as Edrissi's work became known, includes detailed topographical information about such distant locales as England, the Black Sea, and Russia. It was completed in 1154, the year Roger died of angina.

The Norman kingdom would survive another forty years under Roger's son, William I, and his grandson, William II, until as a result of dynastic intrigue it fell to Henry VI Hohenstaufen, the Holy Roman Emperor. Henry's son, Frederick II Hohenstaufen, would rival the Norman kings with his polymathic abilities, cosmopolitan court, and administrative reforms. But after that in Sicily there would be no more golden centuries of which Virgil writes.

❧

The morning of Valentine's Day we treated each other to glasses of *vino vecchio,* a sweet, tawny wine, then proceeded through a park with masses of date palms to Roger's palace, built by Palermo's Arab emirs before he overhauled it. We passed through a series of baroque rooms, furnished in later centuries in a style meant for the flutter of piano keys and the wailing of violins. Roger's bedroom was covered in gold-glass tesserae, with mosaic pictorials of trees and animals more elaborate than the mosaics I had seen in the museum in Sousse.

A massive loggia led to Roger's personal chapel, the Palatine, consecrated on Palm Sunday, 1140. Maupassant wrote that walking into the Palatine Chapel is like entering a jewel. Beneath an Islamic stalactite ceiling are rows of Byzantine icons and Latin inscriptions. The icons of the prophets, of Christ Pantocrator and the Virgin Mary, are austere and stylized. The chapel's deliberate excess expresses the confidence of a universal civilization at the zenith of its power: a time when Moslem seamstresses embroidered Christian texts in Arabic letters for the ceremonial robes of a Norman king; when, as Norwich informs us, the fleet admiral was Greek, the bishop of Syracuse an Englishman, and the bishop of Agrigento a Hungarian. It was easy to be impressed with the builders of this chapel. How certain they must have been in their beliefs! Such a contrast with my own country at the time, its confidence racked by the after-effects of an oil crisis and the Vietnam war.

Palermo's Norman churches, with their Islamic-style tulip domes and severe Romanesque towers, were stunning composites of restraint and sensuality, standing out amid the baroque excesses of the city. In the cloister garden of San Giovanni degli Eremiti ("St. John of the Hermits"), all Arab arches and slender Romanesque columns, I felt I was back in Sidi Bou Said. Here the distance between Sicily and Tunisia dissolved. Roger had built this church in 1142. Although it was adjacent to his palace, he settled it with an obscure group of Benedictine ascetics to demonstrate his independence from the Pope in Rome. The garden was fragrant with palms, cacti, jasmines, orange blossoms, and geraniums. You almost expected Puck, Peaseblossom, and the other fairies to jump out of the greenery. In *The Kingdom in the Sun,* Norwich describes San Giovanni's madder rose domes as "gigantic pomegranates" and notes, "They are not beautiful; but they burn themselves into the memory and remain there, stark and vivid." In the shadow of those five "pomegranates" (they could just as well have been the tops of minarets) we ate fruit and talked about something I no longer remember. I recall only that the cloister's slender, fungus-stained columns provided a fleeting awareness of the eclecticism of early-medieval Islam: a template for the absorption of Greek, Roman, Spanish, Jewish, and other cultural influences. It was a time when Islam was a cosmopolitan rather than a stifling force.

Just as Tunisia, an Arab country, stoked my interest in Roman history, Sicily, a Catholic land, filled me with a desire to learn more about Islamic history. In the Moslem Middle East one sees Islam as it is; in Sicily I saw it isolated in time, in its true glory, preserved within layers of Byzantine and Norman stones.

For example, there was the twelfth-century castle built by William I, Roger's son, called La Zisa, from the Arabic *al-aziz,* "the splendid." Inside La Zisa, *muqarnas* hang from the sides of the dome and merge with geometric tiles to enfold the surviving patches of a fresco: nude bodies appearing like snapshots from the past. Nearby are inscriptions in Arabic, Hebrew, Greek, and Latin, and rows of amphorae decorated with Arabic lettering. Here was the Middle East before the decrepitude of the waning Ottoman centuries and the strains of twentieth-century modernization, which would turn Islam into an austere ideology. And what better picture frame for it than a Norman palace! La Zisa soared into the sky in spare perfection. In its dynamism and symmetry, I compare it now to the Turkish-Persian tower of Qabus in northeastern Iran that I would see many years later. Both La Zisa and the tower of Qabus are reflections of different medieval civilizations, distilled to their essences through fine architecture, with an effect that is surprisingly modern and abstract.

⊙⊙

The best memories grant solace against what the English critic Alan G. Thomas calls the "strap-hanging" toil of middle age. No image of Palermo is as vivid to me as that of the cloister at Monreale: an enclosed garden of thin columns and twin arches, whose rhythmic harmony makes them seem to float, even as they glitter with gold leaf and black and lava-red tiling. Each capital has a different design: of leaves, a lion's paw, a rosette . . . I recall the details because it had been so cold so much of the time, yet in the cloister the sunlight gleamed off the limestone walls of the great cathedral, providing warmth as if it were spring already.

Like the Palatine Chapel, Monreale Cathedral is a store

house of civilizations, in which Orthodoxy, Catholicism, and Islam coexist through the medium of art. William II—the fair-haired and mild-mannered "William the Good"—the last great Norman king, began building Monreale in 1174. The Virgin Mary, it was said, had appeared to him while he was deer hunting, and divulged the location of a treasure: a place where he should show his thanks to God. Thus, he built Monreale. Of course, William had a political reason, too. He needed to create a new archbishopric close to Palermo to check the rising power of the city's prelate, Walter of the Mill (Gualtiero Offamiglio). Monreale would be a Benedictine abbey over which Walter—the Pope's representative in Norman Sicily—had no control. The ramparts and tower of Monreale Cathedral represented secular power: protecting an earthly kingdom against the papacy.

☙❧

Following the reign of William the Good, the Sicilian crown passed through the hands of the Holy Roman Emperor and the Pope, then returned to another group of Frenchmen, the Angevins, whose rule would turn out to be less enlightened than that of the Normans. That is the history you recall in the cemetery of Santo Spirito, near which teenagers nowadays play rough games of soccer.

Moments before vespers on the night of March 30–31, Easter Monday in 1282, the square in front of the Church of Santo Spirito was filled with talking and singing. A group of drunken French officials in the Angevin occupation force arrived, and the faces in the crowd turned cold. One of the Frenchmen, an army sergeant, began bothering a young

Sicilian woman, whose husband stabbed the sergeant to death. When the Frenchmen tried to avenge their comrade, the Sicilians fell on them with the swords and daggers they carried under their cloaks. As the last of the Frenchmen fell, the bells in the square tolled for vespers.

Word now spread throughout Palermo and a massacre erupted against the Angevins. By the next morning, two thousand people lay dead and rebels controlled Palermo. Within a week, there were uprisings in Trápani, Corleone, Caltanissetta, and other towns. Four months later, taking advantage of the rebellion, the Spanish Aragonese navy arrived to challenge Angevin rule. The Angevins, who at the time controlled Tunis, Albania, and Jerusalem, and had designs on Constantinople, suddenly faced disaster. Roger de Loria—inside whose fort I had sunbathed a few weeks before on the Tunisian island of Djerba—carried the Aragonese navy to one victory after another against the Angevins. Fighting continued for years. Then, in 1298, the Angevins, with the help of Pope Boniface VIII, bribed Roger de Loria away from the Aragonese, making him lord of Djerba. But the Angevins were still unable to retake the island. In 1302, a treaty gave Frederick of Aragon control of Sicily, and all Angevin troops withdrew.

The consequences of the Revolt of the Sicilian Vespers were ultimately more dramatic for the Vatican, the chief supporter of the Angevins in Sicily: the revolt was part of a series of calamities for the medieval popes, which would include their so-called Babylonian captivity at Avignon, and which led, in the words of historian Steven Runciman, "through schism and disillusion to the troubles of the Reformation."

·8·

SICILIAN JOURNEY

I was rarely so happy that winter as I was when I found myself on a Sicilian train, anticipating the next arrival. Each journey lasted a few hours, and midday would invariably find us en route. Pungent smells of cheese, salami, and fresh bread filled the carriages as lunches were unwrapped and shared. Tears flowed on crowded little platforms as the train stopped in various towns, where passengers fell into the arms of friends and relatives or said their goodbyes, coming and going from factory jobs in northern Italy.

The journey from Palermo to Agrigento took us through the heart of the island. Beyond the window was an endless whirl of green fields carved up by ravines, with vineyards, fruit orchards, and almond trees. Clay-roofed villages, crowned by churches, stood on limestone ridges. The influence of the

human hand had made a rugged terrain into an ordered landscape. Dark pines and cypresses added a note of introspection; just as agaves and banana trees added the wild flavor of
a savannah, particularly as we crossed into the southern part
of the island, where some vistas were so sharp and barren that
they appeared almost biblical. Date palms, brought by the
Arabs, crowded among trellises and discolored walls. Even in
the bloom of the mid-winter almonds and wildflowers following the rains, there was the drowsy intimation of dust.
How vast and variegated Sicily must have seemed to the first
Greek colonists!

ೋ

We found a damp hotel room in the medieval town. It had
no heating, toilet, or hot water, just a cracked sink and a
view of the Valley of the Temples from the window by the
bed. Before the broad seascape was a dusty tableland, striped
with olives and other cultivation, falling away over an
immense distance in a series of ledges. Here and there on an
outcropping was a finely shaped ocher cube: a Greek temple
too far off to make out the details.

In Agrigento I discovered a book, *Sicily: An Archaeological Guide: The Prehistoric and Roman Remains and the Greek
Cities* by Margaret Guido. With maps and absorbing histories
of each town, it would make a useful companion to Thucydides as the years went by. From Guido I first learned that
Agrigento (the Greek "Akragas") was founded in 581 B.C. by
settlers from Gela, a town forty miles to the east along the
southern coast of the island. Like the other Greek settlements
in Sicily, Akragas was ruled by tyrants: some good, some

bad. Without a stable means of government, the early Greek settlements were prey to individual ambition, so that tyrannies which in Greece itself had already given way to democracy were reborn here. The rule of a single man was further consolidated by the building of temples, requiring vast amounts of both money and organization.

From the window of our room I saw the remnants of ancient city walls that were built by Akragas' first tyrant, Phalaris, who in the mid–sixth century B.C. extended Agrigento's territory through successful wars against the Carthaginians and the native Sicels. Phalaris roasted his enemies alive inside a brass bull that, through some mechanical manipulation, made a roaring sound whenever the victim writhed in agony. His cruelty later caused him to be censured by the ode poet Pindar.

Pindar visited the court of another Akragantine autocrat, Theron, whose "good deeds to others outnumbered the sands on the sea-shore," according to the poet. Theron made a brilliant alliance with Syracuse that led to the defeat of Carthage in 480 B.C. at the great battle of Himera in northern Sicily. Carthaginian prisoners built some of the temples I could see from my window. By the end of Theron's rule, Akragantine territory extended throughout much of Sicily.

Fantastic wealth came with the expansion. Pindar calls Akragas "the most beautiful of mortal cities." Margaret Guido writes that the citizens enjoyed their wealth with "almost nouveau-riche exuberance." They made abundant use of gold and silver, slept in ivory beds, and built expensive tombs for their pets, especially their horses. The city became famous for the opulent sofas and cushions produced by her slaves: even soldiers slept on soft pillows, a symbol of the luxury that brought about its eventual decline.

Akragas remained neutral in the great war between Athens and Syracuse, in the hope that both sides would exhaust themselves. But once Athens had been defeated, the Carthaginians, sensing a power vacuum, invaded western Sicily. As it turned out, Akragas' sudden wealth made it both generous and naive. After the Carthaginians had wiped out Selinunte, Akragas' citizens, at public expense, gave food and shelter to the thousands of refugees, while leaving their own defense in the hands of mercenaries. The Carthaginians bribed the mercenaries and sacked the city in 406 B.C. Rather than fall into the hands of a looting enemy, many citizens gathered in the temple of Athena, to which they set fire in a mass suicide.

The nouveau-riche Akragantines were the ultimate pagans. They glorified not God but man himself. Because man-in-the-flesh was central to Greek religion, the after-life was insignificant. The Akragantines enjoyed earthly pleasures to the fullest. They were concerned with *now*, not the hereafter. It made them generous toward the Selinuntine refugees, even as it did not deter their heroism when they themselves were about to perish.

Returning a quarter century later to Agrigento, I recalled instantly the heavenly light; the fresh, almost-morning smell of the air as I awoke from a late-afternoon siesta; and the crowded, serpentine Via Atenea, filled with restaurants, cafe-bars, and boutiques: all of which made for a sybaritic dynamism that seemed faithful to the materialistic spirit of the ancient city.

෨෧

The first morning we had slept late and treated ourselves to cappuccinos and pastries in a bar before taking a short bus ride to the archæological museum, located halfway between the town and the Valley of the Temples. The collection of Greek pottery is one of the world's finest: case after case of massive, wide-necked *kraters* for stirring wine, and two-foot-tall, narrow-necked amphorae for storing it, as well as for holding grain and honey. Most of the pottery is from the mid–fifth century B.C., Greece's golden age, which saw the democratic reforms of Pericles, the wars of the Greek city-states against Persia, and the Peloponnesian War. They showed epic scenes of soldiers leaving for battle, the intimacies of small dinner parties and symposia, mistresses being dressed by their servant girls, and musicians entertaining. There were scenes of startling sensuality—satyrs catching young women writhing in their chitons, men and women bathing, and Dionysian spectacles. The fixed expressions were always in profile, symbolic more than realistic. Because of the limitations of the style and the smallness of the surface area, like the Roman and Byzantine mosaics I had seen earlier in my journey, the scenes on these vases left much to the imagination. They were the opposite of television, which, because it shows everything, reveals nothing.

There was, too, a marble statue of a Greek warrior, sculpted sometime between 480 and 475 B.C., the period of the Greco-Persian wars. All that remains of this statue is a helmeted head and torso. The arms are missing and, except for part of a thigh, so are the legs. Yet the statue evokes all the horror of the *Iliad*. It captures the process of falling, mortally wounded, in a manner that takes one's breath away. The torso, full of vigorous muscular mass, shows a contracted abdomen. The eyes seem set for one last effort before death. Nearby was a small white marble statue of Aphrodite, who seemed to be wringing her hair after a bath, even though she lacked an arm and was headless. When I returned to Agrigento in middle age, these statues were like the recovered spirits of brief, lost friendships: those with whom I had had a conversation in a hotel lobby or a railway station, whom I had known for only a few minutes or an hour, yet who had said something significant to me. These remnants of antiquity were retrievable in a way that other parts of my past were not.

We walked farther downhill into the plain where the temples lay. The Greeks of Sicily built on a grander scale than in Greece itself, much as early American structures were often larger and more spread out than their British cousins. The Temple of Zeus offered a panorama of devastation, with lizards darting over crumbled columns ennobled by lichen. Cacti punctured the soil in the spirit of naturalistic violence. A seven-meter-long limestone *telemon* lay on its back, its hands behind its head: these atlases had supported the roofs of the temples, like bodyguards around a vault. They have no parallel in the ancient world. Carthaginian prisoners from the Battle of Himera labored decades to build the temple of Zeus. When it was nearly completed, their countrymen flattened it along with the rest of Akragas.

A few hundred meters away was the Temple of Concord, a Doric behemoth that survived the Carthaginian destruction, and was saved by its conversion into a Byzantine church in the sixth century A.D. The columns, metopes, and cornices, strafed by the wind and rain over the millennia, resembled rotting cork. In Greece the white marble temples, denuded of their original paint, appear to us at least as a testament to noble ideals: in Sicily the apricot-colored limestone suggests the voluptuous earthen handiwork of the potter, so that Greek temples in Sicily seem closer in spirit to the Roman ones in Tunisia than to temples in Greece itself.

We walked along the walls of the ancient city, collecting shards that littered the soil, and dreaming of buying a house in Italy—the naive, impractical dreams of young people everywhere. Around one in the afternoon, we hitched a ride back to town and found a *trattoria* for lunch. The sun was unusually strong, so we ate outside. I had *pasta con le sarde,* with anchovies and onions. The local wine came in a colorful ceramic pitcher. A television was turned up loud in the nearby kitchen, where, under fluorescent lights, the proprietor's family was finishing its meal. Among the countless little luxuries I enjoyed that winter was that of getting a bit drunk in the middle of the afternoon, knowing that I could lie down soon after. The ideal picture of the Mediterranean—that of a cafe table in the warm sun, with a harbor in the background—was not easy to come by. The weather was usually cold and rainy, the awnings rolled up, cafe tables packed together closely inside. When the weather was warm enough to sit outdoors, it was doubly appreciated, mortared against time by some detail or other: a particularly friendly waiter, a kitten hunting for leftovers, or, as on one occasion, a wedding ceremony on a nearby beach that began just as we

sat down for coffee. That afternoon in Agrigento is embed-
ded in my memory by nothing in particular, except that it
was part of a perfect day that ended with an evening stroll up
and down crowded medieval streets, followed by a late
evening meal and an Eddie Cantor movie in English with
Italian subtitles, which we watched with our coats on in the
freezing, tumbledown lobby of the hotel.

After a quarter century Agrigento changed drastically. It
was over-built, teeming with poor neighborhoods and luxury boutiques, with Arab and African immigrants selling
handicrafts on the streets and hustling near the railway station. On my visit a quarter century later I had a mobile
phone to keep in touch with work, so that during the
evening stroll I was preoccupied. Travel is most rewarding
when you are young, before a career takes hold—with all the
mistakes and unintended consequences; or when you are old,
and enough is behind you so that acceptance of what has
happened becomes a simple necessity, and you have the freedom once again to think about nothing except the immediate landscape.

❦

Leaving Agrigento by train and heading northeast into
Sicily's poorer, mountainous interior, the sea and palm trees
disappeared and we were embraced by darker vegetation and
solemn, overcast skies. It was as if the rotating earth had
stalled at twilight, just at the moment that the street lamps
go on.

Caltanissetta, an Arab settlement overrun by the Normans in 1086, evoked a medieval fortress, haunting and iso-

lated, displaying every hue of basalt and charcoal, with the dome of the cathedral the blue of a gas flame. Broken roof tiles rattled in the wind as we discovered streets like narrow gorges smelling of olives and salami, their scabby, lignite-darkened facades mellowed here and there, and obscured beneath balconies and oppressive clouds. The damp, icy cold of our hotel room made meals a blessing. We ate lunch in a windowless restaurant with vinyl table cloths. Brown cabinets and dim oil paintings crammed the gray walls. The local wine was a dark, blackberry red. The steaming soup was filled with bits of sausage. We walked back to the hotel and passed one of the makeshift altars lining the street: a gold-painted virgin in a cheap glass case filled with flowers and burning candles stuck in sand. Old women stopped and crossed themselves before it.

The bad weather in the interior made us impatient to move on. The morning we left Caltanissetta a mist was evaporating, so that the landscape of central Sicily revealed itself in stages, like islands in a receding, opalescent tide. We headed southeastward on a bus to the town of Piazza Armerina. The road followed the crest of a mountain chain, a barren geometry of salt and sulfur deposits along ridges lined with umbrella pines. As I stared at mountains and mesas, Sicily assumed the dimensions of a continent.

ର୨

The Roman villa at Casale, outside Piazza Armerina, lay in a valley of poplars, hazelwoods, and fruit orchards under rotting winter rains, permeated by the dense, mildly asphyxiating smell of pine dust. True affluence is a matter of owning fine vistas, so as to appropriate for yourself nothing less than the beauty of the earth. This estate, so perfectly situated, may have been owned by Maximian, one of Rome's co-emperors after Diocletian, in the late third century A.D., had subdivided the empire. Maximian was of Balkan parentage, from the border lands of present-day Hungary and Yugoslavia. According to Gibbon, he was a rustic in both appearance and manners: war was the only art he professed.

The extent and range of the mosaics make this villa the most important Roman ruin in Sicily: many were executed in Sicily by Carthaginian craftsmen or in Carthage itself. But they were a disappointment compared to the mosaics I had seen in Tunisia. One panel showed ten girls in bathing suits doing gymnastics. Even with their flesh exposed, the girls had the antiseptic look of cheerleaders, while the scenes of hunting, banqueting, and chariot racing exhibited a cold and overwhelming pomposity. Though not every mosaic dates from Maximian's era, it seemed the home of a general who had resided in the barracks too long during his rise to the emperorship and, consequently, was deficient in taste or humanity. The place had the aura of the circus rather than of the temple.

But the very opulence of these mosaics—with their fine, technical compositions—inspired its own respect. Rome, like it or not, dominated and suffocated everything else. The landscapes of Africa and the Caucasus that appear in some of the panels, and the animals being transported to Rome that appear in others, testify to the extent of Roman power. There was no soul to any of it, though. I remember a mythic giant in one of the tableaus, writhing in pain, extracting arrows from his body, a scene of particular brutality.

❧

We arrived in Piazza Armerina on a Sunday afternoon, after a brief stop at the Casale villa. The streets were crowded, with children in Lenten carnival costumes. Piazza Armerina rests on three hills. Like Caltanissetta, it was established as a fortress by the Arabs, "Saracens" as they were known to medieval Europeans, after which it was conquered first by the Normans and later by Spanish viceroys, who are responsible for its baroque exuberance. As we climbed each hill, the clay rooftops, dulled to ash by the sun and rain, fell away in trapezoidal formations. Every balcony and staircase was crowded with urns which in warmer weather would have been filled with flowers. The mute, roof-rattling cold made each prospect worth toiling for.

The windiest, coldest point was the piazza beside the Duomo, empty except for a few old men and a couple embracing in overcoats. A few streets away, I remember a woman in a black cape leaning against a nearby wall under moonlight, as though she were posing for one of those elegant portraits by John Singer Sargent. How did the rundown beauty of these alleyways come about? It had been a long process of wars, conquest, poverty, interludes of peace, and, most of all, decay. In the morning I opened the louvers in the room and enjoyed Piazza Armerina one more time.

❧

An hour changes everything, the time it took to hitchhike from Piazza Armerina southward through grape and wheat fields to Gela, on the island's southern coast. We were picked up by a man we had met in the crummy hotel in Agrigento and who recognized us. His name was Fernando. He was a traveling salesman from Rome, marketing orthopedic ware in Sicily, Calabria, and Sardinia. He was well-dressed, over-weight, and enjoyed talking about food. He was driving to Gela that morning because of a good restaurant there.

In place of the picturesque medieval towns of the interior we found a ratty waterfront hub of commercial activity, smelling of salt, petrol, and garbage, reminding me of Marseilles. Gela was dominated by oil rigs, auto and tire shops, and bleak, unfinished apartment blocks. Hordes of men gathered at night around bars as tacky as those in the hilltop towns were elegant. Yet Gela was the warmest and friendliest place we found in Sicily. The local police allowed me to use their typewriter to write an article. In a palm and oleander grove strewn with rubbish by the sea, I remember a young couple frantically making out on a park bench.

Gela, a fast-buck, oily backwater of a town without charm or tradition, is among the oldest Greek cities in Sicily, established in 688 B.C. by colonists from Rhodes and Crete. Akragas had been founded by the citizens of Gela. It was a local tyrant, Gelon, who, unhappy with the sloping beach that formed the harbor here, conquered Syracuse in the early fifth century B.C. and turned it into one of the great ports of antiquity. Gela was the place to which the playwright Aeschylus retired—his grave later becoming a place of pilgrimage for writers of the era. Shortly before his death he wrote the *Oresteia* here. Following a few days of warming myself in the mild winter sun, doing little except hanging about the beach and the port, and successfully locating a typewriter, I resolved to read the *Oresteia* trilogy again, though it had made little impression on me in college.

ೠ

The train ride to Syracuse on Sicily's eastern seaboard lasted several hours. There was the usual bustle upon boarding the train before we took our seats and gave ourselves up to the silence of unfolding vistas. At Modica, I recall three generations of Sicilians—an old man, his son in uniform, and a little girl—all waving goodbye to a relative with tears and kisses. As we slid by other dusty and forlorn stations—ivy-topped ruins with fake Greek statues—I saw how landscape is like a new friend you meet on the road, with hard and soft edges, whom you will soon desert for another; a summary of the historical ordeal of a people.

In Syracuse, it was a short ride to Ortygia, the heart of the city since antiquity. A drooping appendage to the mainland that helps form Syracuse's Great Harbor, Ortygia is an island less than a mile long and half a mile wide, separated from the city proper by a narrow channel spanned by a bridge. Rarely have I been to a place so instantly likeable: a toy town of low buildings where you could see almost from one end to the other, consecrated by the smell of fish and brine, and the hiss of the sea. Ortygia boasts the singular attribute of a good harbor: that feeling of perfect security while one can hear all hell break loose close by. Of all the places I have been in Sicily, Ortygia has changed the least. Hemmed in by water, its streets retain the coziness of a small neighborhood. Even now, particularly in winter, it maintains still the ambience of a sleepy, seedy island village. The sundrenched stone buildings capture you with their chemical colors flickering off the water in the harbor: the runny reds of iodine and vermouth; the blues and yellows of cobalt and tangerines. The elliptical and mullioned windows were like so many fantastic eyes and smiling faces. Black cobblestones lined the streets; espaliers the rooftops. The curved iron balustrades remind me of a Wallace Stevens poem about how a barber's work lasts but a moment—these balustrades were like the finest curls preserved for all time.

಄಄

Syracuse and its environs, at their peak in the late fifth century B.C., constituted a city-state of several hundred thousand inhabitants, perhaps the largest in the classical world. Founded in 733 B.C. by colonists from Corinth, attracted by a fertile valley, a sheltered harbor, and a nearby island with a freshwater spring, Greek Syracuse remained independent for over five hundred years, until 212 B.C., when it fell to the Romans in the Second Punic War. Syracuse's history rivals that of Athens itself in richness, as if the entire record of the Byzantine or Ottoman Empire had been squeezed into one town in Sicily.

Syracuse's greatness began when Gelon transferred the seat of his power here from Gela, and then, with the help of Akragas, defeated the Carthaginians in 480 B.C. at Himera. This was the first heavy blow to Punic prestige. It ushered in a time of prosperity that led to the construction of temples and a port complex. Gelon was succeeded by his brother,

Hieron I, who patronized the writers Pindar and Aeschylus. It was in Syracuse where Aeschylus wrote *Prometheus Bound* before passing his final years in Gela. Hieron was succeeded by another brother, Thrasybulus, a tyrant so cruel that his death was still being celebrated two centuries later. Such tyrants built Syracuse into a power that aroused the concern of Athens. The result was the Athenian invasion of Sicily, chronicled by Thucydides, which culminated in the destruction of Athens' fleet in Syracuse's harbor in 413 B.C.

Though victorious, Syracuse had been weakened severely by its war with Athens. This weakness led Carthage to invade Sicily. Dionysius I, who ruled from 405 to 367 B.C., built the siege walls around the city that protected it during four subsequent wars. Dionysius had a golden bed that was guarded by a special moat and drawbridge. When his courtier Damocles pronounced Dionysius the luckiest man alive, Dionysius allowed him to taste the life of a Syracusan tyrant. He had Damocles feasted as well as ravished by beautiful women, but always with a sword hanging over his head, suspended by a hair. "Now you know what my life is like," Dionysius told the terror-stricken Damocles.

Another tyrant, Dionysius II, had his uncle Dion invite Plato to Syracuse, in order to advise him in the ways of a philosopher-king. But Dionysius II drove Plato away with his brutality, and a disgusted Dion chose to topple his nephew. But rather than a philosopher-king, Dion turned out to be a mere waverer, a hair-splitting intellectual unable to resolve the contradiction between his high ideals and the realities of power: so Dionysius returned as an even fiercer tyrant. He was succeeded in 343 B.C. by Timoleon, the most beloved of Syracusan rulers, who rebuilt many of the nearby Greek towns destroyed through war and neglect.

I learned also about the brilliant-but-cruel Agathocles, who decades later attacked Carthage across the sea and almost saw Syracuse destroyed as a consequence. I became dizzy from so many stories, a confused pageant of names and incidents, of which two dramas stood out: the great naval battle between Syracuse and Athens that led to the failure of the Sicilian Expedition, and the fall of Syracuse to the Romans two hundred years later.

The fall of Syracuse had been preceded by the rule of Hieron II, a general who had risen through the ranks and reigned forty-one years, longer than any other local tyrant. He played Carthage off against Rome, and commissioned the scientist and mathematician Archimedes to design war machines and siege engines for the city's defense. Hieron II kept Syracuse at peace, enriching and beautifying it. He died at ninety, just as the Second Punic War broke out, and was succeeded by his grandson, Hieronymus, a boy of fifteen.

Whereas his grandfather had throughout his long rule worn the clothes of a common citizen, Hieronymus dressed in imperial finery. Succumbing to the machinations of his aunts and their husbands, the spoiled boy led Syracuse into an alliance with Hannibal's Carthaginians, just at the time when the Romans were about to attack the surrounding towns. The besieged Carthaginians, now desperate to rule Syracuse directly rather than through Hieronymus, had two of their agents stab the young tyrant to death. Ensuing mob violence led to the assassinations of his aunts and their husbands, who were blamed for the disastrous policy and the

consequent anarchy never known under Hieron's wise dicta-
torship.

The Carthaginian faction in the city retained the upper
hand, giving the Roman general Marcus Claudius Marcellus
no choice but to attack. The siege dragged on for two years,
stretched out by the catapults, grapnels, and other ingenious
devices that Archimedes had designed for the defense of the
city. Finally, in 212 B.C., after the Carthaginians had been
weakened by a malaria outbreak, a traitor opened one of the
gates into Ortygia, allowing the Romans to pour in.
Archimedes died in the attack. In *The War with Hannibal*,
Livy writes from the vantage point of two centuries later:

> When Marcellus stood on the heights of Epipolae and
> looked down at the city below him—in those days the most
> beautiful, perhaps, in all the world—he is said to have wept,
> partly for joy in the accomplishment of so great an enter-
> prise, partly in grief for the city's ancient glory. He remem-
> bered the sinking, long ago, of the Athenian fleets, the two
> great armies wiped out with their two famous commanders,
> and the perils she had passed through with all her wars with
> Carthage. He saw again in fancy her rich tyrants and kings,
> Hieron above all, still vivid in men's thoughts. . . . As all
> these memories thronged into his mind, and the thought
> came that within an hour everything he saw might be in
> flames and reduced to ashes, he determined on a last effort to
> save the city.

Alas, Syracuse was sacked and its Greek treasures brought to
Rome. But even as Greek culture in Sicily began to decline,

this first, dramatic encounter with Greek art began an era of intellectual ferment in Rome that would not be replicated until the Renaissance. It is the fall of Syracuse, more than any other event, that signifies the end of the Greek era in classical history and the beginning of the Roman one.

ᏩᎽ

The urban landscape of Ortygia exquisitely expresses this dense and layered past. Ancient Greek ruins lay in pits beneath the cobblestones, surrounded by remnants of medieval churches. The heart of this compact magic was the Temple of Athena, fronting a semi-circular plaza of faded baroque palazzi, grimy with mold. The temple—a fifth-century-B.C. Greek ruin inside a medieval church—looked so mortared over and rebuilt that it was like a totem to history itself: a piled-up wreckage of styles and epochs. The Doric temple had been Christianized in the seventh century A.D. and later turned into a mosque, before being reconsecrated with Norman and baroque retaining walls. The entrance was a massive, double-tiered portal, behind which was a second entrance of twisted columns. Inside, gargantuan, time-battered columns built by the pagan Greeks were overlaid with statues of medieval Virgin Marys, with Romanesque archways alongside. I felt deep within the marrow of religious faith that is the driver of history. How can human events be based purely on reason, I thought, if the faiths that built this house of worship were motivated by such violent passion? An enthusiastic English woman beside us kept repeating the word "palimpsest" to describe the building.

The Temple of Athena and the other grand facades of Ortygia, though demanding vast squares, often faced narrow alleys that appeared even narrower on account of the snaking fruit stands and overhanging balconies encrusted with flower pots. Some of them led out to the swishing waters of the Great Harbor, which on winter evenings sounded like the inside of a seashell. The oval-shaped harbor, seemingly calmed by the masts of sailboats, was a wonder: vast enough to imagine the great naval battle that had occurred here in the summer of 413 B.C., yet small enough to encompass one's imagination of it. At dawn, dusk, or on a cloudy afternoon, the harbor becomes a leaden vat, reminding us that it is a mass grave of warriors, their bones long ago dissolved in a gray silt of time. Heroism, the reputation of generals and statesmen, and the fate of empires disappear in its alluring emptiness.

You could almost hear the crash of the triremes at dusk. Sleek vessels, invented in either Phoenicia or Egypt, triremes, according to the military historian Victor Davis Hanson, could travel at great speed, powered by the oars of 170 sailors. But the trireme was also unstable, capable of capsizing abruptly and spilling its entire crew into the water as soon as it was hit lightly by another ship. The island of Ortygia curved around the harbor, forming a narrow opening where—by lashing a line of triremes together with iron chains—the Syracusans had blocked the escape route of the Athenian fleet. There were two hundred triremes fighting each other in this harbor, as the Athenian general Nicias went from ship to ship encouraging his men. Nicias' defeat was historically pivotal: the failure of the Sicilian Expedition undermined the morale of the home front in Athens, and played a role in Sparta's eventual victory in the Peloponnesian

War. That led, in turn, to Persia's domination of the ancient world, to be followed by Alexander's conquest of Persia.

⍟

One afternoon, we finished a liter of wine over lunch and sat in a delicious stupor looking out at the harbor, taking turns reading an out-of-date English newspaper at a restaurant by the Aretusa Fountain, an ancient freshwater spring where, legend says, Artemis converted her handmaiden Aretusa into fresh water to protect her from the designs of a river god. Espresso did not cure our sleepiness as we watched ducks flop amid palms and papyrus in the fountain, as they have for centuries. Finally, with the sun low in the sky, we went for what we thought would be a quick excursion to a tourist office and a grocery store.

At the tourist office we met Robert, an elderly landscape painter with a long white beard who told us that he had lived for twenty years in Brazil, traveled just about everywhere else, and returned to Syracuse the day before by ferry from Malta. Robert spoke Italian, was a vegetarian, and seemed otherwise to be in a daze: all of which seemed to qualify him to me as a legitimate eccentric artist. His credentials were completed by his admission that he was staying at the youth hostel.

Robert took us to the apartment of his friend Giuseppe, another elderly artist, who showed us his paintings and played the reel of a documentary film he had made about the local theater festival. Robert and Giuseppe inundated us with clever talk about art, theater, and the history of Syracuse over glasses of cheap whiskey that seemed to us a luxury.

As talented and learned as each man appeared, and as naive as I was, I was nevertheless struck by their poverty, their lack of recognition, and their abject loneliness, demonstrated by their need to impress two young travelers. I did not want to end up like them. For a moment in Giuseppe's apartment I was terrified that I was wasting time traveling aimlessly about the Mediterranean, without a job or prospects to return to. I had to do something, I told myself. But I hadn't a clue what.

☉☉

In a thirteenth-century palazzo in Ortygia one picture stood out. The other paintings spoke of an airy idealism: a world of stiff, one-dimensional figures and landscapes, in which every person and background was a symbol. But this one painting showed people as they actually were, dirty and lonely: here was a more credible spirituality. The painting that I saw that morning was "The Burial of St. Lucy" by Michelangelo Merisi Caravaggio.

Caravaggio was born in 1571 in northern Italy. In the words of the art historians Catherine Puglisi and John Rupert Martin, Caravaggio revolutionized painting with a terrifying, snapshot realism: a belligerent rebuke to the idealized logic of Greek statuary. Like that of Velázquez, it was said that in his time Caravaggio's art was "not painting, but truth." Caravaggio smashed canonical models and introduced human passions such as fear, hatred, misery, and lust into his paintings just as his English contemporary Thomas Hobbes was doing something similar in philosophy. A brawling, swashbuckling figure, Caravaggio was at home in the street: he killed a man in a dispute over a tennis match, stabbed another in a fight over a woman, wounded a soldier, beat up a fellow painter, and threw food at waiters and stones at guards in Rome. He solicited no disciples, but his influence was enormous. Caravaggio became the pioneer of a raw baroque naturalism that was based on a sensational sensuality and a theatrical use of light. He partially, albeit intensely, illuminates his subjects out of deep shadows, so that they have the volume of sculptural reliefs. With Caravaggio there can be no light without darkness. With him the distance between the painting and the viewer collapses. It is as if we are inside the picture itself. In this painting in the museum in Ortygia I saw a muscular turmoil and naked-before-God pathos that brought me back once more to Rodin's garden.

It was as if Caravaggio was leading a one-man charge against the barricades of polite opinion. Caravaggio arrived in Sicily by ship from Malta in October 1608, fleeing murder charges. Here in Ortygia he painted "The Burial of St. Lucy." In early 1609 he fled onward to Messina, where he painted "The Resurrection of Lazarus" and "The Adoration of the Shepherds." He moved next to Palermo, before escaping to Naples in late 1609. Sicily's ancient ruins, rock quarries, and catacombs inspire his darkly majestic backgrounds.

I looked at the painting a long time. It was darker and browner than the glossy reprints I would see later in art books. All of the figures were lost in a confusing netherworld of shadows, with soil and arched walls blending together. Only the hairy, muscular thighs of the grave diggers stood out. Life's squalid majesty, with its sufferings and exertions against fate, was captured here. St. Lucy, the patron saint of

Syracuse, lay dead on the ground. The priest's ruby robe offered the only rich color on the canvas, and even that was grimy. But because everything enveloping the robe was darker still, I could appreciate it all the more. The first sight of that Caravaggio was like entering a darkened room: you had to wait until your eyes adjusted to the light in order to make out the details.

ϾϿ

As the train left Syracuse heading north, Mount Etna came into view, its slopes scarred with snow, soaring to nearly eleven thousand feet. Dominating the landscape of eastern Sicily, Etna seemed less a mountain than a god. Virgil writes in the *Aeneid* that it

> rumbled and flashed,
> Formidable in eruption. . . .
> She vomited rocks and brought up lava streams.

The rocks that Etna vomits up are said to be those thrown by Polyphemus and the other Cyclopes in Homer's *Odyssey.* Just as the story of the Cyclopes could be a metaphor for the anarchic conditions that the first Greek settlers encountered in Italy, it could also be a description of Etna in eruption. The Mediterranean world ends somewhere up the slopes of Etna, where the landscape of human cultivation stops and there is only a molten, prehistoric emptiness.

We alighted at Taormina, a resort that in the 1970s was already beginning to fill with German holidaymakers and priapic hustlers. The lovely little train station, located by the water, was paved with expensive mosaics. As the bus ascended to the town, crenellated palazzi crept out of the rock while palms and cypresses—tall, elegant dowagers—danced in the wind. Through the mist, Etna occupied the entire horizon. Despite the tour groups, Taormina had a jet-set feel, with the kind of scenic backdrops that only money could buy. The parks and gardens were like drawing rooms, overseen by faded terraces crowded with geraniums and bougainvillea and caressed by vines along crumbly walls. Twisting alleys housed fancy, overpriced cafes. Old churches were kept company by expensive jewelry stores. The principal tourist attraction was a Roman theater with thin madder stones, whose foundation was laid in the third century B.C., perhaps by the Syracusan tyrant Hieron II. The landscape that fell away from it was composed of sculpted rock and campaniles, with a seascape and volcano in the distance. In Taormina, you felt like a character in a movie. The place offers the illusion of success even if you have yet to achieve anything. Observing the young backpackers who still flock here twenty-five years later, I don't think I was that unique.

En route north to Messina, the Italian mainland swept into view across the narrowing, aquamarine strait. Destroyed by World War II carpet bombing, Messina was a drab glacis of cheaply constructed, post–World War II buildings, utterly charmless. A letter waiting at poste restante informed me that a travel article I had written about the holy city of Kairouan in Tunisia had been rejected by *The New York Times.* Messina's art museum was "closed for restoration"; it would be years before I would see the two Caravaggios there. I was bored and depressed as we walked along bleak boulevards to the twelfth-century Norman cathedral to see the noontime chiming of the clock tower. Six carousels, some with life-sized gold figures—angels and knights, horses and charioteers, and fair ladies—all began to turn in sequence on the squat gray campanile, topped by a four-sided tower. Bells pealed. Then a dragon roared and a cock crowed. Finally, the fair ladies bowed as the delightful music stopped, and I realized that my time in Sicily had come to an end. With much of my money depleted, I fell asleep as the rail car rolled into the black hull of the ferry, transporting us in the middle of the night across the Strait of Messina to mainland Italy.

## HADRIAN'S VILLA

Nothing that I saw in mainland Italy affected me as much as Hadrian's Villa in Tivoli, east of Rome, near the foothills of the Apennines. In her fictional autobiography, *Memoirs of Hadrian,* Marguerite Yourcenar writes that for the second-century-A.D. Roman emperor, a single, blissful morning in Athens left a deeper impression than the fifteen years he had spent in the army. The morning I spent prowling around the ruins of his villa, after sleeping at an adjacent campground, left a similar impact.

In the 1970s there was not the rash of ugly buildings around Tivoli that there is now. The ruins of the villa, twice the size of those of Pompeii, lay off the road, unannounced, on small tufa rises of orange soil, amid ancient olives, cypresses, and sculpted pine trees, with water trickling from pools and fountains. It rained intermittently. I took shelter under the half-collapsed domes and vaulting, and in underground chambers. I read later that in 1803, Chateaubriand had visited the villa and had also been caught in the rain, taking refuge in the same places. "The fragments of masonry were garnished with the leaves of scolopendra," he wrote in his description of his journey, "the satin verdure of which appeared like mosaic work upon the white marble."

The reticulated stones inset in the mortar of the walls, thick with wet moss, had blended together into one vast and beautiful accretion, in the way that generations and their particular dramas blend with past and future ones, leaving patterns only: like different varieties of earth. The floors with their rich and muddy carpet of tesserae were a lesson in geology. The fragments of slate and marble parquetry offered colors subtler yet. I remember a lone pillar so dark that it was like a diseased and veiny elephant trunk.

Shattered domes revealed clouds moving overhead in countless visions of eternity. It was a place made for silence and for contemplation, where you wanted a book handy. Every corner was a cloister. No view was panoramic: each seemed deliberately composed. For Hadrian, writes Eleanor Clark in a 1950 book, *Rome and a Villa,* the availability of water was more important than a dominant view.

Hadrian's Villa was the Versailles of the ancient world. In the remnants of apsidal niches, vestibules, colonnades, and pools, one can detect signs of an arranged grandeur absent in the Roman Forum, a mere warehouse of ruins in comparison to Tivoli. And while so much of Maximian's villa in Casale spoke of vulgarity, here everything appeared more refined. Scholars compare the villa with Thomas Jefferson's Monticello because the scenery in each place has been so deliberately managed. The villa was Hadrian's personal project to the same extent that Monticello was Jefferson's.

Hadrian, whose aromatic voice Marguerite Yourcenar transmits across the millennia, observes,

> The Villa was the tomb of my travels, the last encampment of the nomad, the equivalent, though in marble, of the tents and pavilions of the princes of Asia. . . . I turned toward the realm of color: jasper as green as the depths of the sea, porphyry dense as flesh, basalt and somber obsidian. The crimson of the hangings was adorned with more and more intricate embroideries; the mosaics of the walls or pavements were never too golden, too white, or too dark. Each building-stone was the strange concretion of a will, a memory. . . . Each structure was the chart of a dream.

Eleanor Clark calls the villa Hadrian's "memoir," more complex than that of Proust, re-creating the strands of the emperor's life. Hadrian was the ultimate collector; he needed everything—every book, every sculpture and alcove—to remind him of some cherished moment from his own past: "My hidden study built at the center of a pool in a Villa is not internal enough as a refuge; I drag this body there, grown old, and suffer there," reflects Yourcenar's Hadrian. The circular mini-island surrounded by a moat, to where the emperor retreated, sings of innovation and Greek purity with its slender Ionic columns in curvilinear patterns. Greece inspired sophisticated Romans like Hadrian just as

Europe has inspired many Americans. But it was water that Greece lacked, and here Hadrian supplied it.

In the words of Yourcenar's Hadrian, one's true birthplace is where "for the first time one looks intelligently upon oneself." Youth is "a formless, opaque, and unpolished period, both fragile and unstable." It is over-rated: for in youth one is prone to such fads as the barbarous cult of Mithra, to which Hadrian was attracted as a young soldier. A homeland may be not a place but a book, or a brief memory.

To his villa, Hadrian brought thousands of books purchased in the course of his travels. (His bibliophilic interests extended even to Athens, and to the library there that bears his name.) The villa's library, Greek statuary, and landscaping re-created for the aged emperor the experience of his earlier wanderings. It was a monument to Hadrian's spirit and intellect, the way Freud's library was to his. Sheltering a lamp flame in his hand, Hadrian would pause, perhaps, before a sculpture of Praxiteles, while remembering his dead lover Antinous, a male youth a quarter century his junior who had drowned in the Nile on a journey with him.

It is the Canopus that I remember best from my first visit, a long pool with narrow hairpin turns, shaded by pines and cypresses, named after a point on the Nile where a canal joined up from Alexandria. Ammianus Marcellinus, a Greek historian writing in Latin in the fourth century, would call that spot in Egypt "most delightful because of its beautiful pleasure resorts, its soft air and healthy climate, so that anyone staying in the region believes that he is living outside of this world." Hadrian honored that Egyptian setting with this pool, where he held his late-night parties. Lining the water are caryatids, Roman copies of classical Greek statues, and a veiny marble crocodile reminiscent of ancient Egypt. Because all the statuary faces the water, you see the sculptures only from the opposite bank, so that the dominance of each is reduced and they merge organically with the view. You can lose yourself watching the fallen leaves group themselves into tiny islands in the water. Again, as everywhere here, it is the scene that you recall more than any of its individual elements.

Hadrian is thought to have been born in 76 A.D., in southern Spain, to a family of Roman settlers. He was a protégé of the emperor Trajan, his father's cousin. As a young man of barely twenty, Hadrian served in the Roman military in the Balkans and at thirty-one he rose to the rank of governor of Lower Pannonia (modern-day western Hungary and eastern Austria). Later he was an archon, or chief magistrate, in Athens, where he acquired the philhellenism that would mark the rest of his life. When Trajan, on account of illness, returned home from the East, he left Hadrian in command of his army and made him governor of Syria. There, in 117 A.D., Hadrian's soldiers proclaimed him emperor upon learning of Trajan's death. A traveler at heart, described by the Roman theologian Tertullian as "an explorer of everything interesting," in 121 he began a four-year tour of the empire that took him to Gaul, Germany, Britain (where he built the frontier wall that bears his name), Spain, North Africa, Greece, the Balkans, and Asia Minor. He climbed Mount Etna en route home through Sicily. In 128 he began another four-year journey, this time through the Levant: from Greece to Egypt by way of Asia Minor and Syria.

Hadrian was the first Roman emperor to grow a beard. Here, too, he copied a Greek fashion. He was an enlightened ruler by the standards of the age. The scholars William L. MacDonald and John A. Pinto write that "he ameliorated the conditions of slaves, forbade castration, and on the whole was an alert responsive ruler for whom the rule of law was almost always the final authority . . . in the unending, depressing story of absolutism, he stands well back from the threshold of damnation."

Like all rulers, Hadrian wanted to give the world form and order. You can imagine him wandering about the grounds, besieged by aides—preoccupied with the power struggles in Rome, the building of his wall in Britain, the difficulties of establishing security in the frontier zone of the Middle East, and dealing with the rebellious Christians and Jews who in his mind were the enemies of progress. History is about the characters of great individuals. Tivoli grants a visual insight into one of them.

# DIOCLETIAN'S PALACE

The Adriatic was where I first felt the indefinable differentness of the Orient. Alone now, hitchhiking eastward from Tivoli through the whirling, deforested Apennines, I arrived in Pescara, where there was a campground near the port. The boat the following day to Split, in Yugoslavia, did not leave until the late afternoon, and by the time I had crossed 125 miles of sea at 20 knots per hour, it was past midnight. Walking down the gangplank at the edge of the harbor in Split, the wind in my ears, I was chilled by its lonely linearity: a panel of black water meeting a sweeping flagstone expanse, with railway tracks peeking through low, shed-like buildings. An India-ink belfry stuck out against the bruised sky. The street lights indicated a feeble, unsteady electric current.

I noticed a sign, IZLAZ ("exit"). The spray of mysterious Slavic consonants from the passport and customs officials that I heard against a backdrop of swaying palm trees was like doors smashing open: at that moment I wanted never to return to school. Instead, I just wanted to keep moving eastward and northward. The attraction of this language was less its beauty than its strangeness. Continuing along the harbor toward the town, I found a small park where I spent the night on a bench. A mild wind provided the sensation of enfolding warmth, as though everything and everybody around me were friendly. It was because of that night that I remember the last lines of Auden's poem "The Traveller":

> The cities hold his feeling like a fan;
> And crowds make room for him without a murmur,
> As the earth has patience with the life of man.

Daylight revealed a nomadic encampment of molded plastic stalls where old clothes were being set out for sale. Mountains—the Dinaric Alps—rose in the background along with high, ancient walls: those of the Roman emperor Diocletian's Palace, which circumscribed the old quarter of Split. I left my rucksack at the *gardaroba* at the railway station and had a breakfast of weak tea and poorly stirred scrambled eggs shiny with grease, in a hotel where brown machine-made carpets had been laid on the walls, illuminated by chocolate-colored brass fixtures in faux-medieval style. It was my introduction to the exotic drabness of Tito's communism, which I would later learn to recognize in the overuse of pebbly concrete, weedy and forlorn parks, groups of women in smocks cleaning the streets, and cafeteria-style restaurants that, except for the Turkish coffee in brass beakers, had the institutional flavor of prison mess halls. Communism, even Tito's variety, was an Industrial Age feudalism that despite its Central European antecedents had elements of Asiatic despotism. In Sicily, North Africa beckoned. On Yugoslavia's coast, the Balkans and Asia did. In Sicily, the cultural potpourri was confined to the archaeological sites, the churches and museums; the modern reality was indisputably Italian. Here the mix of civilizations was omnipresent and particularly thrilling: while the hotel revealed a brutal stripping away of tradition, it nevertheless faced a square straight out of Venice, with twin arches and a beautiful terra-cotta facade. There was a wildness about Split, a sense of one world beginning and another ending.

I wandered to a park, littered with ruins and mantled by cedars. The sound of church bells cracked the air. The moldy northern wall of Diocletian's Palace stretched before me, seven feet thick and fifty feet high, scarred by the scrub growing from its crevices and broken every so often by arched windows that had been bricked up long ago. The stones had come from the nearby island of Brač, which would furnish the stones for the White House in Washington, D.C., some fifteen centuries later. They got smaller and more anarchic in their arrangement as my eyes crept upward. It was history in progress: the Roman period topped by Byzantine and later ones. Diocletian had not been its only inhabitant—it had also housed Julius Nepos, the next-to-last Roman emperor in the West, who had fled here from Ravenna following a coup. He stayed for five years before being slain by his own soldiers. I walked through a grandiose gate and fell instantly into canyon-like alleyways, their stones blackened with age.

It was then that I came upon the Peristyle, the ceremonial gateway to the imperial quarters. The alleyway I had been following ended abruptly in a submerged flagstone expanse. On three sides I saw columned Roman buildings over which medieval Venetian ones had been built. I felt as though I had entered a brilliant salon of, well, *History,* the only word I could come up with at the moment. On my left was a line of six dull pink granite columns from Egypt, supporting a frieze and acanthus the color of bleached bone, charred in many places. Resting on a pedestal between two of the columns was a cracked, black granite sphinx that Diocletian had, along with the columns themselves, brought back from Egypt. Also to my left, behind the six pink columns, were twenty-four massive octagonal pillars, enclosing Diocletian's mausoleum and temple complex. In the seventh century A.D. the mausoleum had been converted into a cathedral, and a Romanesque belfry had been added in the late Middle Ages: the one I had seen the night before against the dark sky.

To my right as I entered the Peristyle from the narrow alley, imbedded between another line of columns, were Romanesque and early-Gothic palaces whose lintels and balconies had been blackened and eaten away by the salt winds. And straight ahead of me as I entered was the Protiron, the monumental entrance to Diocletian's private apartments, where the emperor had stood to receive homage from his subjects: four columns supporting a triangular gable, with two chapels from the sixteenth and seventeenth centuries behind it. Broken stone slabs littered the vast area. Byzantine crosses had been etched everywhere.

My head felt light, my legs a bit wobbly from the fitful night on the park bench. I stood there dumb, not knowing really where I was, convinced I had wasted my life up to that point. A few laborers in dull smocks, their faces unshaven, were sitting at a cheap cafe sipping Turkish coffee by a line of stalls. Otherwise, I was alone. Split might as well have been Samarkand for me then.

"First experiences should be short and intense," John Julius Norwich has observed. A visit of only a few hours to Venice as a sixteen-year-old later inspired him to write a two-volume history of the city: it was a visit he "can still feel—not remember, *feel* . . ." Gibbon recalls that it was while "musing amidst the ruins of the Capitol" in Rome in 1764, listening to "the barefooted friars . . . singing vespers in the Temple of Jupiter," that he resolved to write *The Decline and Fall of the Roman Empire.* Gibbon and Norwich— as great as they are—were not the first tourists, or the last, to be so overwhelmed by a storied site as to want to learn how that grandeur came into being.

❦

If Hadrian was a romantic aesthete who encouraged the arts, Diocletian, who ruled the Roman Empire 150 years after him, at the turn of the fourth century, was a nuts-and-bolts pragmatist who spent most of his life in military camps. The marble busts of Hadrian suggest the brooding self-absorption of a philosopher; those of Diocletian the command-and-control stare of an auto company executive. The less interesting and enlightened of the two, Diocletian, "a good bullying soldier," in Rebecca West's phrase, was nevertheless as great an emperor, and a humbler one. If Hadrian bears comparison in his intellect to Jefferson, Diocletian might be Eisenhower, or Truman.

Gaius Aurelius Valerius Diocletianus was an Illyrian born in Salonae, a few miles from Split. According to Gibbon, this first emperor from the Balkans "was more illustrious than any of his predecessors," and, having ably reorganized Rome after a sustained period of incipient anarchy, may be considered "the founder of a new empire." Realizing that Rome (which encompassed the entire Mediterranean world, in addition to much of northern Europe and the Near East) was too vast for one man to rule anymore, upon becoming emperor in 284 A.D., Diocletian divided the throne four ways. While he himself settled in Nicomedia, in western Asia Minor, to watch the East, he made Maximian, another Illyrian, responsible for the West, and established a new capital at Milan. Some years later he further subdivided the two halves of the empire, giving Galerius control over the Balkans and Constantius I Chlorus control over Spain, Gaul, and Britain. To this tetrarchic structure were added new categories of administration, buttressed by new pomp and ceremony—exorbitant in cost even as the tetrarchy restored domestic order. The secrecy and mystery that was a hallmark of Byzantium actually had its origins in Diocletian's court in Nicomedia. Diocletian's restitution, while impressive, was a balancing feat that prolonged, rather than arrested, Rome's decline. Rebecca West writes:

Diocletian had been born too late to profit by the discussion
of first principles which Roman culture had practiced in its
securer days; he had spent his whole life in struggles against
violence which led him to a preoccupation with compulsion.

The end of his reign was clouded by the last great persecution of the Christians. The persecutions were, in fact, carried out by Galerius, the ruler in the Balkans—Diocletian's
vow not to spill blood went unheeded. The result was a
resurgence of martyrs' cults, such as Donatism in North
Africa, followed by Christianity's own conquest of the
empire soon after. In 305 A.D., following twenty-one years in
office, Diocletian voluntarily abdicated the throne, with
Constantius and Galerius, two of the tetrarchs, succeeding
him. He spent the last nine years of his life at the vast palace
he had built for himself in Split. It was an example that no
previous emperor, and few subsequent emperors or Catholic
popes, would follow. Though illness may have had something to do with his decision, it showed nevertheless the wisdom and humility of a man whose soldierly experience and
sense of duty more than compensated for his lack of learning.

❧

I crossed the flagstone expanse and walked up the steps of the
Protiron, to the reception hall of the imperial apartments: a
large, barrel-vaulted chamber of thin bricks, stripped bare of
its mosaics and with its dome open to the sky. I went next
inside the cathedral, once the emperor's mausoleum, which
exuded a similar feeling of military strength. The dome of the

cathedral, a moving yellow-gray hue, was wonderfully bare and smudged with the smoke of ages. Adjacent to the cathedral dome were the tombs of two bishops: composites of classical and medieval styles, they were visual demonstrations of a historical continuum that made antiquity feel less far away and, therefore, less mystifying. The entire palace area, in fact, conceived by Diocletian as a Roman camp and filled in with houses and alleyways throughout the Middle Ages, became for me, in the course of subsequent visits, the history as told through architecture of a long and magnificent seaboard.

Dalmatia, "land of mountains," is the name used for the Adriatic coast of what is now Croatia: part of the former Yugoslavia. It is also the name of a tribe, the Delmata, which declared independence from the rest of Illyria (the ancestor of modern-day Albania) and organized itself along this coast. In the late fourth century B.C., the establishment of Greek colonies nearby by the Syracusan tyrant Dionysius the Elder led to Roman incursions here. But it was only after its conquest of Syracuse in 212 B.C. that Rome turned its attention in earnest to the Adriatic's eastern shore, this time to counter pirates and Macedonian kings who had aligned themselves with Carthage. Two centuries of warfare followed, as Rome also tried to subjugate the Delmata and other Illyrians. Finally in 9 A.D., after yet another Illyrian revolt, a fed-up Tiberius abruptly concluded an armistice in Bohemia, and along with his nephew Germanicus he traveled south to crush the uprising. "From that year," writes the historian Giuseppe Praga, "Dalmatia settled down submissively in the shadow of the Roman eagles."

The downfall of Rome in the West in 476 A.D. led to rule by Gothic barbarians until Justinian annexed Dalmatia to the Byzantine Empire in the early sixth century. But Dalmatia's coastal position and its distance from Constantinople made it difficult for the Byzantines to control local politics. In fact, they barely tried. Nevertheless, the Byzantine cultural influence, a variation of the Roman one, persisted, and it was only in the second decade of the seventh century that classical civilization truly ended here: the consequence of a Slavic invasion. That is when Split (Spalato) was settled. As the Turkic Avars and Slavs came down from the Dinaric Alps and destroyed the nearby Greco-Roman city of Salonae, the part of the Romanized population that managed to survive fled to the off-shore islands. Some later took refuge in Diocletian's Palace, which had been abandoned the century before. The refugees sub-divided the imperial suites, as well as the living quarters of the former Roman slaves, servants, and soldiers. Streets and alleyways formed and thus was laid the basis for medieval Split.

In Dalmatia's case, the invading Slavs were Croats, a people streaming westward out of the Carpathians. But Dalmatia's language and culture remained heavily influenced by Latin, and ties to Italian cities like Ravenna continued to strengthen. The elite families, known as *maiores,* were also influenced by the cosmopolitan refinements of Constantinople. From the ninth through eleventh centuries, Split was nominally a Byzantine city. By the tenth century, though, as Byzantium came increasingly into conflict with Venice, the Romanized inhabitants of the Dalmatian coast sought Venice's protection against both Byzantines and Croats, the latter of whom had recently turned to piracy. The anti-pirate expedition along the coast here, launched by Doge Pietro Orseolo II in May 1000, laid the basis for Venice's "Empire of the East." A maritime trading power, imperial Venice could be relatively liberal, and the city-states of Dalmatia would often play it off against the land-bound empires of first Hungary and later Ottoman Turkey. Twelfth-century Split illustrates Dalmatia's confused, chaotic situation. The historian Praga writes,

> The city had passed under the sovereignty of Byzantium, which had managed to enter the good graces of the people to the extent that the citizens demanded that the archbishop pay homage to the [Byzantine] Emperor. The influence of Slavic squires spread all around. Manichean, Catharist, and Patarin heresies swarmed over their land. . . .

Yet through it all, Roman Catholicism triumphed. Dalmatia's Catholicism, writes the historian Fernand Braudel, "was a fighting religion, faced with the threatening Orthodox world up in the mountains and with the immense Turkish peril." Dalmatian galleys helped the Venetians destroy the Turkish fleet in 1571, at the Battle of Lepanto, off the western coast of Greece, one of the greatest naval engagements in history. Soon afterwards, Split became the principal Venetian port for trade with the Balkans, with warehouses and merchants' lodgings built adjacent to Diocletian's Palace. In 1797, the fall of Venice to Napoleon shifted the balance of power in the region. Austria, with Napoleon's consent, filled the political vacuum here. But from 1808 to

1813, the French ruled Dalmatia directly, building new roads as part of a modernization program that ended with Napoleon's downfall. Then came a century of Austrian mis-rule until the collapse of the Habsburg Empire in 1918, when the mixed Slavic-Italianate population of Dalmatia joined the new multiethnic state of Yugoslavia.

In the 1970s most of this history was invisible to me, not only because I was young and ignorant but because Tito's communism helped make it so: burying much of the cultur-ally eclectic Adriatic tradition under a sterile carapace of state socialism. The nasty tribal wars of the Yugoslav succes-sion that followed the collapse of the communist security structure in the 1990s further distanced Dalmatia from its coastal, Italianate roots, as Split became deluged with Croat-ian refugees from the Bosnian interior, people whose out-looks were constricted by horrific experiences. But in 2002, when I last returned, with boats coming and going from Italy, elegantly dressed people rushing about, new jewelry stores and pricey boutiques opening in the shade of Diocle-tian's walls, grocers offering imported cheeses and salamis, and deep rows of cafes along the embankment, I felt as though I had never left Sicily. The bleak and lonely quay area, where decades before I had arrived for the first time, now boasted colorful signage announcing travel agencies and a mini-mall with a cybercafe. Globalization in Dalmatia was expressing itself through an Italian prism. Rather than dull the ambience, it was returning Split to its original Adriatic origins as a whirlpool of different cults and civilizations. The sea, busy with ships, was wonderfully *present,* a liberalizing force. As nearby Slovenia rejoins Central Europe, Dalmatia is returning to the fold of Greater Italy, a cultural taxonomy only because of the inexorable submergence of the Italian state within the European Union.

◌◌

A few miles from Split, in an industrial zone crowded with factories and garages, I saw a Roman aqueduct that had been used to transport water from the ancient city of Salonae to the spot where Diocletian chose to build his palace. The water came from a natural spring at the foot of the Dinaric Alps, unruly fastnesses capped by long, granite ridges which protected the Dalmatian coast from the worst ravages of the fighting in the 1990s. The site of Salonae had been perfectly chosen by the Syracusan Greeks in the fourth century B.C. It was near this spring, along the quiet, willow-braided banks of the Jadro River, in sight of the sea. In 2002, I revisited the archaeological remains with a Croatian friend, a former diplomat of the now-defunct Yugoslavia. Marred by highways and a cement plant that hadn't been here when I had first seen it three decades earlier, Salonae still does what an archaeological site is supposed to do: it inspires silence and reflection that, in turn, can often lead to memorable conversation.

The dense fabric of ruins provided a rich mineral base for flowers and grasses. Chamomiles were sprinkled like fairy dust. Rows of Byzantine-era pillars supported a blooming vine trellis. My friend and I walked along the top of ancient Salonae's northern wall, bordered by the aqueduct. Spread out beneath us were the ruins of a basilica and of public baths from the fifth century A.D. Figs and olives formed a lacy green background, screened by fog. My friend had served in Yugoslavia's embassies in both Iran and India. In 1992, he and his wife had fled here from Belgrade during the civil war with only two suitcases, leaving a comfortable diplomatic life behind. They were lucky to be taken in by relatives. Surrounded by the tapestry of ruins and vegetation, we talked of Diocletian's icy practicality, unburdened by airs and absent of nuance, and how this was not a bad trait for a war-time leader. I mentioned that America, like late-third-century-A.D. Rome, abounded with military might. And if American peacekeepers in nearby Bosnia were replaced with European ones, it would be an ironic result of that military superiority. The United States, I explained, thinks it has the luxury to loosen its bonds with the rest of NATO, while projecting power unilaterally in the Greater Near East. Offloading its imperial responsibilities in the Balkans was a way for America to make its European allies useful, given that many European countries lacked the means or the desire to help track down Islamic warriors in Afghanistan. But my friend feared that America's absence on the ground in Bosnia would mean more influence for the French, who had at times cooperated with Serbian war criminals. "At the top," he said, "the governments in Croatia and Serbia are much better than they were a few years ago, but below the highest levels it is the same old criminal gangs in power that led us into the war. The liberal Italian influence in Split is growing, yes, but the influx of soldiers and refugees from Bosnia-Herzegovina will set us back for years." He added, "You had some good diplomats who finally stopped the killing here, but the situation is more fragile than you think. The worst consequences will result if the U.S. deserts the region." The vast tableau of a ruined city made us historically aware to a degree that we wouldn't have been otherwise. The ruins were like a burden on our consciences.

໑໑

On my first visit to Split, tired and dirty I had wandered into the old city from the palace's northern gate. I remember glancing briefly at a greenish bronze statue in the park of the tenth-century Croatian patriot, Bishop Gregory of Nin. The bishop's sharp nose, pointed cap, claw-like fingers, and determined, narrowing gaze showed a distorted angularity: like that in Greek icons imbued with religious nationalism. There was the force of Rodin without the universality of suffering that graces his work. The sculptor, Ivan Mestrovic, was the product of a nation that had yet to firmly establish itself in this turbulent frontier zone—he needed to be a Croat in a way that Rodin had no need to be French.

Mestrovic was born in 1883 in a nearby mountain village, and at fifteen he was apprenticed to a stonecutter in Split. So apparent was his talent that a wealthy Austrian paid for him to go to Vienna to study art. There he befriended Rodin, and under Rodin's influence, he moved to Paris, where in 1908 he rented a studio in Montparnasse. Abroad, Mestrovic's activities on behalf of an independent South Slav (Yugoslav) state that would bring together Croats, Serbs, and Slovenes made him an enemy of the ruling Austrian Habsburgs. His statue of a Croatian bishop of Zagreb, Josip Strossmeyer, famous for his enlightened attitude toward the Orthodox Serbs, is a demonstration of Mestrovic's own liberal views. Mestrovic returned home following World War I, when the new kingdom of Yugoslavia was born out of the carcass of the Habsburg Empire. But the outbreak of World War II and the installation of a fascist regime in Croatia led to his imprisonment and subsequent exile. When the communists came to power he sent many of his works back to Split, but he never lived there again.

In the garden of the Mestrovic museum in Split, overlooking the Mediterranean, are a collection of bronze female nudes that show a private, more cosmopolitan Mestrovic missing from his public monuments. Like Rodin, Mestrovic can communicate an entire concept through a simple gesture. "Hope": the bust of a woman craning skyward, eyes closed, hands clasped. "Job": a skeleton breaking loose from a body in unbearable anguish. "Seated Woman": similar to Rodin's "Old Woman," except here there is only sadness. Mestrovic, because of where he was from, and the times in which he lived, lacked the luxury of Rodin's indulgences. Still, in this garden you can sense his humanistic ideals breaking down the boundaries of time and place.

## DUBROVNIK RISING

Dalmatia is a barer, more sun-drenched Maine, with the same wonderfully shattered coast, thick with island masses and in late winter, as in Sicily, almond trees in bloom, punctuating a canvas of olives, agaves, figs, and artichokes. Culturally, it can be maddeningly difficult to pigeon-hole, with Italian and Central European Habsburg influences, as well as the more unkempt features of the Turk and Slav. Here, in little off-shore harbors painted by sunlight, you can find the heavy cuisine of Hungary served under palm trees.

Trogir, a squiggly medieval town surrounded by sea, half an hour north of Split, typifies the pleasantness of this coastline. It is full of cafe tables and dramatic vegetation: brooding hemlocks, poplars, date palms, and flowering judases. In Trogir I felt as though I could walk on water, with the mainland on one side and a larger island on the other, both linked by small bridges. The glassy channel is a light marble blue, drawing in so much sunshine that it nearly erases the communist-era detritus of factories and wrecked cars on the horizon, restoring the landscape to some imagined innocence. The red-tiled roofs and cigar-toned facades reflect like jelly in the water. Fancy marinas flank stalwart fortresses. There is the ever-present smell of seaweed. The Croatian spoken here has the same teasing lilt as the Serbian spoken in Kotor and the Arabic of Beirut: somehow the seaside softens languages. Walking along the quay in Trogir, sipping a brandy that the waiter gave you gratis after you finished your meal and bottle of wine, watching sailboats glide across your line of vision, is to be reminded of Henry Miller's famous line upon entering the Greek island of Poros by boat: "To sail slowly through the streets of Poros is to recapture the joy of passing through the neck of the womb. It is a joy almost too deep to be remembered."

Trogir's architecture exists courtesy of the Venetian Renaissance. It was Trogir and other similarly beautiful Dalmatian towns that first enlivened my interest in Venice: that Italian city-state with a Byzantine personality, whose history is as dense and crowded with intrigues as those of Constantinople and Syracuse, and whose political and social cohesiveness—a feature of its small, water-bounded urban geography—gave it the luxury of a limited democracy through an elected oligarchy that lasted over a thousand years. Without being a police state, Venice boasted one of history's greatest spy services: its military and security establishment inseparable from its merchant community. The

Venetian Empire, which stretched from Dalmatia to Palestine—and included the Greek Peloponnese and Cycladic islands as bulwarks against the Turks—was won through trade and intelligence-gathering as much as through bloodshed. "Alone of all the states of Catholic Europe," John Julius Norwich writes, "it had never burnt a heretic." Venice was a place of religious toleration, where secular politics reigned in place of the intemperate sanctimony of the popes. The late-thirteenth-century Venetian traveler Marco Polo was likely born on the Dalmatian island of Korčula, halfway between Split and Dubrovnik. Dubrovnik, which I reached after a five-hour bus ride south from Split, is Venice in miniature.

ᏇᏇ

First there is the drama of a climatic fault zone: a Gothic, wintry intimacy—the work of dark oaks and cypresses—set against a glittering, summery sea. Then, as one rounds another cliff wall, Dubrovnik appears almost as a philosopher's ideal of beauty: a compass of rooftops encased within monumental fortress walls that are, in turn, embraced by the sea on one side and by vast drifts of mountains on the other, while in the background lurk ranks of islands.

The Adriatic suggests the outer world. The mainland mountains, with their imprisoned valleys and villages, suggest the narrow ethnic divides of Bosnia and Herzegovina, just a few miles from the shore. Dubrovnik's fortress walls— one hundred feet high, twenty feet thick, multitiered and studded with towers—have defended the city against both imperial threats from the sea and murderous attacks from the interior. The fact that civil liberties necessitate a military strategy is one of several historical lessons that Dubrovnik teaches.

Evening fell, and I approached the Old City on foot. Despite its exquisite little harbor stacked with pleasure boats that looked like toys in the lead-gray water of dusk, Dubrovnik is not picturesque. It is too substantial. Its weather-beaten galleried roofscape speckled with belfries, atop a cluster of Renaissance and baroque walls, like many a medieval fortress town I had seen in Sicily, is a perfect backdrop for Shakespearian drama.

The sky was black. It was a cold March night, and globular lamps illuminated the battlements. As I walked over a drawbridge and inside the Ploce Gate, a statue of St. Blaise—Dubrovnik's patron saint—guarding me overhead in an alcove, I found myself inside a towering gorge: city walls grazed my shoulder on the left and the walls of a Dominican friary did likewise a few feet away to my right. Then the view widened into a plaza framed by the Gothic and Renaissance Sponza Palace and a fifteenth-century fountain. A stone column the shape of a medieval knight stood in the middle of the pavement. Children kicked soccer balls and slipped by me on skates. Old people and young couples walked arm in arm.

Extending from the plaza, as if into infinity, was the Stradun, Dubrovnik's premier promenade of polished flagstones, glittering like glass in the floodlights. Built after an earthquake in 1667, it was lined with cafe tables and identical baroque arcades: a linear time pageant out of a Canaletto cityscape, in which the peal of church bells and the chatter of cafe crowds go back unchanged hundreds of years. I wandered off into staircased alleys and into stores and intimate neighborhood bars. The neat clutter of pavement stones, roof tiles, cafe tables, and framed, gilded pictures bespoke a deeply evolved urbanity absent in the landlocked towns buried behind the mountains that I would see on visits in the years to come. In a pool of floodlit loneliness, I watched a couple emerge and embrace. Dubrovnik was a perfect urban arrangement, crowded at night despite the cold.

Almost every time I looked up I saw a statue of a saint, usually St. Blaise, cradling a model of Dubrovnik in his hand, ready to step off the top of a church and into the air, mingling with the crowd.

And the crowd was so chic and noisy. More than two decades later I would revisit Dubrovnik directly from Zagreb, Croatia's inland Balkan capital of more than a million people, where there seemed to be less chatter than among the few thousand inhabitants of this Old City. But here was Mediterranean dash: men in turtlenecks and trench coats and women in fur-lined coats and black stockings, with operatic makeup and expensive sunglasses, hair gleaming from spray or mousse. On that return visit, also in March, I walked into a shop, open late like everything here, and talked politics with a smartly dressed woman, who told me:

"We are clever diplomats and yearn, perhaps, to be independent again. Since the war began in 1991, we have been ruled from Zagreb. But the Zagreb government is full of Mafia types and Croatian peasants from Herzegovina. We are all Croats in Dubrovnik, yes, but people here crave cosmopolitan living. I miss the well-educated Serbs who used to come here in the summers from the best neighborhoods of

Belgrade. Only low-class people these days are nationalists. If Dubrovnik were once again an independent city-state, we might become rich."

Dubrovnik—a Serbo-Croatian term that may refer to nearby oak forests—was not even the exclusive name of the city until the twentieth century. Before that, for roughly a thousand years, it was the independent, Catholic, seafaring republic of Ragusa. (The word *argosy* means "ship of Ragusa.") After World War I the government of the new Yugoslavia changed the name officially to Dubrovnik because Ragusa sounded too Italian, though the name is putatively Illyrian. Ragusa fought off Saracen sieges and, with the passive encouragement of Spain and the Vatican, constantly slipped away from the dominating grasp of the Venetian, Habsburg, and Ottoman Empires, playing off each against the others. Independent Ragusa was the gateway to the East, where caravans began their five-hundred-mile overland journey through Montenegro, Kosovo, Macedonia, and Bulgaria to Constantinople. Ragusa's naval might insured that it owned warehouses in every major Mediterranean port. Only in the nineteenth century, after the Napoleonic Wars, did Ragusa succumb to Habsburg domination.

Ragusa, Braudel writes, "was the living image of Venice": its merchants were active in all the big towns of the Balkans and the Levant. They dominated the transport of Sicilian wheat and salt across the Tyrrhenian Sea as far as Spain, sending their profits to banks in Naples, Rome, and Venice. Ragusa's neutrality between the Pope and the Turkish Sultan allowed its ships to pass unharmed.

Ragusa employed Enlightenment principles before they

were articulated in Western Europe. In 1389, following the Turkish victory over the Serbs at Kosovo Polje, Ragusans recognized the right of asylum for defeated Serbian princes, even though Ragusa itself was an ally of the Turks. The slave trade was abolished here in 1417, at a time when such a trade was highly profitable in the Mediterranean. The fifteenth century also saw the establishment of a health-care network and free public schools. The sixteenth century gave rise to municipal waste removal and town planning, with little frittered away on ostentation as in Venice: the austere baroque facades lining the Stradun were regulated thus. Nevertheless, this "Whiggish liberalism," as it has been called, was built upon rigid oligarchy, diplomatic deception, and massive defense walls. Ragusa was foremost a mercantile city, and the nobility's progressivism represented the ultimate in noblesse oblige. Indeed, the city's history suggests that such categories as "democratic" or "authoritarian" may be less important than the values of the ruling elite.

The story of medieval Ragusa is a poignant demonstration of how social relations and statecraft are often a matter of the lesser evil, for only by accepting that fact can an outnumbered people defend itself. A caste system divided nobles, commoners, and workers, and intermarriage was strictly forbidden between groups. In *Black Lamb and Grey Falcon,* an encyclopedic account of the history and geography of Yugoslavia, Rebecca West explains that such a system may have been ordained by circumstance:

> The Republic was surrounded by greedy empires whom she had to keep at arm's length by negotiation lest she perish. . . .

Foreign affairs were her domestic affairs; and it was necessary that they should be conducted in complete secrecy with enormous discretion. It must never be learned by one empire what had been promised by or to another empire, and none of the greedy pack could be allowed to know the precise amount of the Republic's resources. There was therefore every reason to found a class of governors who were so highly privileged that they would protect the *status quo* of the community at all costs, who could hand on training in the art of diplomacy from father to son, and who were so few in number that it would be easy to detect a case of babbling.

With only thirty-three noble families in a population said to number in the tens of thousands in the fifteenth century, the city could easily supervise the ruling elite. Ragusa's was a corporatist leadership in which few dominant personalities emerged. The Rector, the equivalent of a prime minister, who wore a black velvet stole over a red silk toga, was elected for only one month and could be re-elected only after an interval of two years. During his month in office he was held prisoner in the palace except for ceremonial appearances. It was a variation of the Venetian system, whose executive power rested to a large extent in the hands of the Council of Ten: a group elected for one year and which, in turn, chose three leaders from among themselves who ruled alternately for a month each.

Though Machiavelli's *Prince* makes no mention of Ragusa, its progressive Whiggish-style government seems a perfect expression of his principles: a cold, aristocratic realism dedicated to self-preservation. Even Ragusa's Catholic fervor was self-interested, securing the support of two great powers, Spain and the Vatican. Nevertheless, had Ragusa's nobles been more tolerant of its Orthodox citizens, they might have secured the help of Orthodox Russia at the Congress of Vienna in 1815, when Ragusa was handed over to Austria. It was never again to be independent.

In the Rector's Palace—a confection of Gothic and Renaissance architecture where Ragusa's rulers held office for their allotted month amid gilded mirrors and blue-and-yellow Neapolitan faience—I couldn't help but be drawn to the portraits of Ragusa's noblemen, with their Italian and Slavic names. Their calculating expressions bespoke a ritualistic conformity; they looked as if they belonged to a monastic order. Years later, between October and December 1991, and again in May 1992, when Serbian shells rained down on the Old City, the fifteenth-century walls and seventeenth-century flagstones, particularly along the Stradun, which had been financed by these crafty entrepreneurs, absorbed many direct hits and shrapnel with remarkably little blemish. In 1998, I took a walk along the top of the fortress walls to assess the damage from the Serbian bombardment.

I looked over hundreds of thousands of clay roof tiles—the true architectural soul of the Mediterranean, expressing what Edgar Degas called "the patient collaboration of time." Like fossils impressed on stone, they formed a record of the seasons: cold, wet winters and scorching-hot summers, creating a patchwork of haunting, subtle hues. There were chestnuts, ochers, glowing siennas, the result of the accretion of salt air and fungal growths over many years. Given enough time, the tiles turned the color of bleached bone and from a distance seemed yellow almost, like lemons. Yet, after a moment of unparalleled splendor, I looked closer:

Many of the tiles were new, so that blotches of flat, tomato red marked the areas where Serb shells had hit, and which subsequently required new tiles, which hadn't yet begun to age. Looking at the depressing homogeneity of color, I thought of how the new Croatian state—at the time an underworld tribal dominion which had emerged from the ruins of the former multiethnic Yugoslavia—was attempting to Croatianize Dubrovnik: subtly transforming it from a cosmopolitan cocktail into a sterile, nationalistic uniformity; its guides and revised tourist literature emphasizing a Croatian past that deflected from the Old City's tradition of political independence and its strong links to Italy and the rest of Dalmatia, rather than to Zagreb.

Dubrovnik exudes eclecticism. I entered the museum of the Dominican friary, where neither a brass-cast flagon from fifteenth-century Nuremberg nor a sixteenth-century Flemish diptych of Christ and the Virgin seemed out of place surrounded by the art of Slavic, Hungarian, and Italian masters, including an angel by Titian. The Dominican church, with empty white walls distinguished by the most elaborate Gothic portals, was like many I had seen in Italy. The fourteenth-century Romanesque cloister of the Franciscan friary was another landscape experience more Mediterranean than Balkan: a stone fountain in the midst of a luxuriant garden with a simple lemon tree. Alleyways were steep and sun-swept mazes graced by orange blossoms and drying laundry.

On my last visit I headed for the Old City's produce market beside the cathedral, a flagstone space bordered by weather-stained baroque buildings, with a triumphant statue of a local poet, Ivan Gundulic, in the center. At one vegetable stand a buxom woman wearing an apron opened a bottle of brandy flavored with medicinal herbs and poured me a capful, then handed me a juicy fig. It was 9 A.M. and the brandy seeped into my head and chest like perfumed fire. She smiled. Every day, at exactly 11:55 A.M., the rooftops surrounding this market fill with pigeons, who wait motionlessly for five minutes until the cathedral bells peal, when they fly off in formation: a Dubrovnik miracle.

Another morning the weather turned colder. The Adriatic was wild and especially somber, suggesting the enigma of Albania to the south and the Habsburg interiority of Trieste to the north. I walked through the medieval-Renaissance stage set of the main square and the Stradun once again, their strong and frugal beauty growing with familiarity. I thought about the bright side of the Middle Ages, which is, after all, Dubrovnik's central lesson: this city and other mercantile city-states drew from rich cultural harvests to preserve their independence, while projecting influence abroad. In a world where urban regions (Catalonia, Singapore, São Paulo) are becoming the organizing principle of economic life, Dubrovnik as an example of an enlightened and independent city-state is relevant anew; as well as becoming the counter-force for the petty nationalisms that still threaten it. In the words of a 1930s shipping poster I noticed in the Maritime Museum by the harbor, this city is still "Ragusa."

That cold morning the outdoor cafes along the Stradun

were full, with seats available only inside. People sat in their sunglasses and stylishly tapered coats, craning their necks toward the pale sun, lingering an hour over their espresso. This is the Mediterranean, where appearance is everything, and warm weather is often a matter of mind. May Dubrovnik always be sovereign.

# MAGIC BOXES OF
# CRACKLING CANDLELIGHT

In Brindisi, in Italy's windswept southeastern outback, Virgil died in 19 B.C. while en route back to Rome from Greece. His great work the *Aeneid* lay unfinished. It was from Brindisi, still a main transit point, that I took a ferry to Greece after returning to the Italian side of the Adriatic from Dalmatia.

The ferry left Brindisi at midnight. At dawn I woke on the other side of the Strait of Otranto, the Adriatic behind me as the boat headed into the Ionian Sea. The wind howled as it had the night before, yet now there seemed to be a soft, whispering quality to it, as if it were imparting a secret. It cleansed the atmosphere to a camera lens sharpness. Greece proclaims itself with a cruel, naked light that, as the late Oxford classicist Maurice Bowra notes, stimulates the sculptor more than the painter. In Greece, even in its luxuriant western islands, colors are less apparent than the stark contours of things. The Austrian poet Hugo von Hofmannsthal observes that Greece "is austere. It rejects all daydreams, even historical ones. It is drab, barren, dramatic and strange, like a terribly emaciated face. . . ."

Each of the fir trees and white buildings that I saw from the ship was isolated against a clear and empty background, recalling the figures I had seen on the Greek vases in Agrigento. "Just as a lack of open vistas in lands thick with tangled vegetation," Bowra writes, "may account for the crowded character of Mayan or Khmer sculpture, which reflect the forest or the jungle in its pullulating pressure, so conversely in Greece open spaces" help to set off each object from the other: so that the emphasis is on the individual rather than on the group. That hallmark of classical Greek thought— and consequently of western civilization—is partly a function of landscape.

Throughout the day the boat tripped south along a screen of islands, whose harbors and limestone contours had the searing, back-lit quality of stage props. I arrived after dark in Patras, from where a bus whisked me eastward to Athens. Charmless and noisy, Athens would, over time, lure me with its familiarity. As my visits piled up, I learned where to go to eat cheaply and well, where to find an air-conditioned library to read, where to get laundry done, where to sell a pint of blood for $20 to offset travel expenses, where the African and Middle Eastern embassies were to get visas for onward travel. In November 1982, I came to Athens for a few days and stayed seven years, as I quickly realized what a perfect base it was for a free-lance journalist wanting an apartment by the sea, a short plane ride from news hot spots like the Horn of Africa, the Middle East, and the Afghanistan-Pakistan border.

Athens' fascination lay not in the Parthenon and other ruins, but in the fact that it was the first of many Third World cities I would encounter over the years. From Paris south to Marseilles and beyond, all the way to Dubrovnik, I had seen planned, historically rooted cities. This was also true of modern-day Tunis, designed by the nineteenth-century French. As for the souks in places like Kairouan and Sousse, like the medieval towns that I saw in Sicily and Dalmatia, they were the outcomes of long-standing communal and architectural traditions; whereas the Third World of the late twentieth century was characterized by the lack thereof. Athens simply sprawled, white hot, with little shade or planning, a disease growth of concrete. From three hundred houses in 1834—the year it became Greece's capital— Athens had swelled to several million inhabitants, because of the influx of refugees from the Greek-Turkish War of 1921–1923 and the Greek Civil War of 1946–1949, and the urban migration of the 1960s that affected much of the underdeveloped world. In the 1970s, Athens prepared me for what I would find later in Cairo, Teheran, and Karachi. While the Greek archipelago was the birthplace of western democracy 2,500 years ago, at the start of the last quarter of the twentieth century, Greece had evolved into a non-Islamic Middle Eastern country.

There were the motorcycles that ran over your feet on the sidewalks and the slumy coffee houses in Monasteraki, out from which the city began to spread in the 1830s, with their cracked mirrors, paste-on icons, and exposed electric wires dangling like entrails, and their old men in dark, moth-eaten suits sucking on water pipes and snapping worry beads as they stared at the filthy walls. There was the old Turkish mosque with conical tiles propped up by luggage shops like a house on stilts. The back wall of the Library of Hadrian gave into a humble stretch of shacks crisscrossed with sagging clothes lines. At cheap, fold-out tables on the sidewalk, I filled myself with lamb and grilled octopus, washed down by the sterilizing fire of *ouzo* and the tang of resinated wine served in cheap, cylindrical cans. There were the bricks of goat cheese drowned in olive oil and blackened with oregano; the olives were brought swimming in vinegar. Largely unchanged through the millennia, Greek food has the force of elemental truth, like the pulverizing light.

The language I found was phonetic and the grammar forgiving—at least on a conversational level. In the local museums, I saw gods depicted as humans; unlike the statues I had seen of Roman emperors, who were depicted as gods. The ancient Greeks, the products of small city-states, individualized everything, whereas Roman statuary evinced the cruder and coercive values of a mass society. André Malraux writes that Greek sculpture looks erotic only when compared to the Gothic nudes with which we in the West are familiar, but when we compare it to ancient Indian sculpture we see that the Greek nude radiates the abstract ideal of freedom.

But it was Byzantium, not ancient Greece, that I experienced away from the tourist areas.

My favorite walks in Athens were along Ermou and

Mitropoleos Streets, buried under boutiques and tall plate-glass buildings. Here and there were tiny jewels of umber-streaked brick and tea-rose marble on the verge of drowning under the chalky mass of modernity. Every evening I followed a stream of Greeks into these chapels, interrupting their journey home from work to light a candle before an icon. In an area of drapery shops on Ermou Street is the eleventh-century Kapnikarea Church, which back in the 1970s occupied a traffic island with honking cars speeding by its entrance. Having dodged the traffic, I would find myself dashing into the Kapnikarea out of breath. It was like passing through an invisible barrier from one world to another. Everything seemed out of focus in the darkness and the mind reeled from the clouds of pine incense and the crackle of beeswax candles. The apse was painted in 1950 by Photios Kontoglou, an iconographer whose work had led to a renewed interest in Byzantine art—the fusion of ancient Greek and Syrian styles to project the values of the medieval church. It was like the grace and simplicity of classical Greek sculpture superimposed on a background of luxuriant eastern carpets. Kontoglou's fresco in the Kapnikarea is of the *Platytera,* the Virgin Mary, arms outstretched in prayer and the child Jesus against her chest. The pallor of her skin and her disproportionately large eyes create a mesmerizing effect. Lime will not hold pigment so well after it dries, so he executed the whole fresco while the lime was wet, working for hours without a break.

For days I walked past Mitropoleos Square and noticed only the ungainly nineteenth-century Cathedral of Athens. Then one day I spotted the other, smaller church—Aghios

Eleutherios—built in the eleventh century on the site of an earlier church, and decorated with a marble facade of beasts and dancing figures carved in relief. The interior was a wonder-work of squinches, barrel vaulting, and quarter domes rising one atop the other, with Christ Pantocrator ("Ruler of All"), eyes aflame, staring down on me from the main dome. There was a sixteenth-century church too on Mitropoleos Street, wedged between the poured-concrete pillars of the Ministry of Education, like a doll house about to be crushed. No more than three or four people could fit inside, yet the interior teemed with icons, censers, and *tamata*—silver plates depicting the afflictions for which invalids seek cures from the saints. I learned years later from a local scholar that this tiny church, named Aghia Dynamis ("the Power of the Holy Virgin"), stands on the site of a pagan temple dedicated to the chthonic power of Herakles.

As with the Peristyle in Split, and other places I had come upon that winter, the real attraction these churches held for me was a vicarious sense of exploration: inside these dark, magic boxes of crackling candlelight I felt myself alone, immersed in different civilizations. In Tunisia, I had become aware of Rome; in Sicily, of ancient Greece; and in Greece, of Byzantium. Byzantium, in turn, led me to an enchanting realm of books that revealed how travel writing, rather than a low-rent occupation for the Sunday supplements, could also be a means to explore art, history, literature, and statecraft: it was in Greece where I began to figure out how to make a living.

# ❦13❧

## LITERARY BYZANTIUM

In *Abroad: British Literary Traveling Between the Wars,* Paul Fussell writes that "the explorer seeks the undiscovered, the traveler that which has been discovered by the mind working in history, the tourist that which has been discovered for him by entrepreneurship and prepared for him by the arts of mass publicity." Thus, exploration belongs to the Renaissance, travel to the nineteenth-century bourgeois age, and tourism "to our proletarian moment," when the masses need a break from the tedium of the work place.

Travel is work. Tourism, by contrast, requires little effort. Fussell explains that

Etymologically a traveler is one who suffers *travail,* a word deriving in its turn from Latin *tripalium,* a torture instrument consisting of three stakes designed to rack the body. Before the development of tourism, travel was conceived to be like study, and its fruits were considered to be the adornment of the mind and the formation of judgment.

From the deserts of southern Tunisia to Taormina and Dalmatia, my experiences that winter hovered between travel and tourism. In the Tunisian outback and in the interior of Sicily I was often cold and uncomfortable, far from tourist crowds and learning about places that had yet to be commercialized. Elsewhere, though, even as I struggled to increase my knowledge of ancient and medieval history, I was doing so in a manner prepared for me by the tourist industry and which involved little ingenuity. That did not make it unrewarding. The fact that there are many places where one can only be a tourist does not mean that such places are without value, or that they cannot inspire at least as much as the classroom can.

I have learned as much as a tourist as I have as a so-called traveler. In the 1970s, I knew young people traveling alone who could put up with the cheapest hotels and the most arduous conditions, yet who were less concerned with learning about the local culture than finding a place to buy hashish; even as I met senior citizens in large groups, staying at antiseptic hotels, who were walking encyclopedias of archaeological sites. Nevertheless, the realization that I was moving about the Mediterranean in an age of tourism stoked my curiosity about a circle of Englishmen who were, in Fussell's view, the last true travelers.

❧

One summer evening in 1927, two Englishmen in their early twenties, Robert Byron and David Talbot Rice, sat on the steps of the guesthouse of the Serbian monastery of Chilandar, on Greece's Mount Athos peninsula, discussing the future of the novel. In his travel memoir of that summer, *The Station: Athos; Treasures and Men,* Byron writes:

> we agreed that if ever a great novel, to rank with Shakespeare, Velasquez, and Beethoven, could be written, it is now. Only now are we learning to probe the unreasoning machinery of the human mind. And now, for the first time, man holds the world in his palm, placed there by mechanised transport. It remains for an artist to leave posterity a picture, not of dialects or tribes, countries or continents, but of the globe of the twentieth century. For the longer the opportunity lasts, the less worth while will it be. Western civilisation is becoming universal, the race a homogeneous one. And before we die, half the variety of the picture will be gone. . . .

Byron could also have been writing about the future of the travel book. Three-quarters of a century later the world is still full of variety, with western civilization only a veneer in many places; nevertheless, the world is much more homogeneous now than it was in 1927, even while the means existed then to go almost anywhere (however slower and less convenient the manner).

Conditions for travel writing may have been more propitious then for another reason: the absence of television and other electronic distractions gave those armed with classical educations more time to read and hone their intellects, allowing some of them to communicate their thoughts in a language particularly exquisite. Here is Robert Byron on the approach to the Greek monastery of Simopetra on Mount Athos: "the building . . . thrusts its triple clump aloft, each incredible facade exaggerating its own perspective to the call of some invisible scene-shifter behind the imminent caerulian canvas."

Though they were children of Empire, writers such as Byron, David Talbot Rice, Freya Stark, Lawrence Durrell, and Patrick Leigh Fermor were generally not concerned with geopolitics. (Indeed, when Freya Stark did pontificate on political trends in the Middle East, subsequent events often proved her wrong.) In this respect, they were different from the nineteenth-century Prussian general Helmut von Moltke journeying through the Ottoman Empire and the young Winston Churchill in Sudan and the Northwest Frontier of British India, both of whom employed travel writing to explore strategy and national interest. Products of the disillusionment following World War I, with its memories of cold trenches and dreary, inconclusive carnage, writers like Byron rejected both the climate and politics of England as they fled to the Mediterranean, the nearest place with a semitropical climate. Only with the outbreak of World War II was Byron, according to his friend Christopher Sykes, delivered "from his foolishly trusting faith in 'the modern spirit,'" after which he "perceived a profounder duty" to his country.

Still, the uncanny ability of these writers to describe a scene resulted periodically in insightful political analysis. Lawrence Durrell's *Bitter Lemons* belongs to a slightly later period. A travelogue about Cyprus in the 1950s, it begins as a romantic account of buying a house by a sea that "banged and rubbed under the moon," and metamorphoses into a study about, among other things, how frustrated young men turn to violence in "an agricultural island being urbanized too quickly." There is Paul, one of Durrell's students, a "thin, solitary" orphan of seventeen, who was "never troublesome in class" and whose school work was "tidy and painstaking," who one day quietly tells the author that freedom must be earned through blood. Aware that the Greek Cypriots "enjoyed almost perfect civic freedom," Durrell observes that, nonetheless, "they had no say in their own affairs from the point of view of popular suffrage," giving their lives "a strange flavour of stagnation." Though the foreign community on Cyprus believed that middle-class Cypriots were more worried about their pocketbooks than about freedom from Great Britain (and consequent union with the Greek motherland), Durrell will have none of this: he explains that after the liberation of Macedonia and Crete, that of Cyprus is "irresistible" from an islander's point of view. In any case, tough tactics usually hurt the innocent as well as the guilty, leading to more resentment and thus more recruits for the anti-British cause. He writes,

> the evil genius of terrorism is suspicion—the man who stops and asks for a light, a cart with a broken axle signaling for help, a forester standing alone among trees, three youths walking back to a village after sundown. . . . The slender

chain of trust upon which all human relations are based is broken—and this the terrorist knows and sharpens his claws precisely here.

And when "you give a chap a mask and a pistol," he will "bump someone he owes money to before getting on with" the business of ethnic killing. Some of Durrell's pages tell you more about the current situation in Gaza and the West Bank, and in the Balkans, than many newspaper accounts.

Such rare bouts of analysis notwithstanding, Byron, Durrell, and the others were primarily aesthetes who understood that the ultimate aim of human existence is the appreciation of beauty. Thus, they paved the way for the best kind of tourism, rather than the worst kind. Byron begins *The Station,* about a summer on Mount Athos, with words that anyone who cherishes antique lands can savor:

> Thither I travel, physically by land and water, instead of down the pages of a book or the corridors of a museum. Of the Byzantine Empire, whose life has left its impress on the Levant and whose coins were once current from London to Pekin, alone, impregnable, the Holy Mountain Athos conserves both the form and the spirit. Scholar and archaeologist have gone before, will come after. Mine is the picture recorded. If patches are purpled with a tedious enthusiasm, or watered with excessive references to the past, let the reader recall his own schoolroom and discover the excuse.

I discovered *The Station,* then already fifty years old, after my visit that winter to Mount Athos. At the end of the book

Byron explains the title. "This is the Holy Mountain Athos," he says, bidding farewell to the reader, "station of a faith where all the years have stopped." A semi-autonomous peninsula in northeastern Greece, Mount Athos is a place where Byzantine life and traditions have been preserved in their entirety. Women have been barred for nine hundred years—not even female animals are allowed. The monks live still by the Julian calendar and the Byzantine clock: midnight coincides with the setting of the sun. On "the Holy Mountain," as it is called in Greek, eight hours a day are spent in prayer, beginning at 8 A.M. Byzantine time (2 A.M. local time in the outside world). Only sand roads connect the twenty monasteries on the thirty-mile-long peninsula, and some of the monks have lived alone for decades in cliff-side caves. Arriving at the monastery of Iviron, Byron writes, "The earth is behind us. Prostrate in the guest-room . . . we lie upon another plane of existence, back in the mysterious, immaterial *regnum* from which the mind cast loose with the Renaissance."

The author's enthusiasm is heightened by the gray English surroundings from which he has just emerged. The "colour" of the Athos environment, he notes, "lives by contrast with my own." Romance, in other words, exists mainly through comparison. Byron was twenty-two when he came to Mount Athos with his Eton friends David Talbot Rice and Mark Ogilvie-Grant, in order to photograph the frescoes in the various churches and monasteries. Because the larger purpose of the journey was to appreciate the art of the Byzantine Renaissance, the group traveled later in the year to the Byzantine fortress of Mistra in the Peloponnese, and then to Crete to see the landscape that had inspired El Greco. Byron believed

that Byzantine art constitutes the true origin of western painting, with El Greco, the sixteenth-to-seventeenth-century
Spanish artist of Cretan origin, providing the link.

*The Station* was a revelation to me. It was a travel book
with a controversial thesis. Byron uses the travel genre as a
mechanism to argue that the legacy of eastern Byzantium is
more important to the West than that of Greece and Rome.
(He delineated this argument further in *The Birth of Western
Painting,* coauthored with Talbot Rice.) His scholarship is
occasionally questionable. His friend Sykes writes that the
virtues Byron "discerns in Byzantium and denies to Latin
Christendom were present in both in some degree, as were
the vices." Byron seems unaware that the "crude" anti-
Byzantine stance of those like Gibbon had already been
abandoned by many scholars. But such things were known
only to specialists, not to a reader like myself. As Sykes puts
it, Byron was a useful *vulgarisateur,* who, through fresh and
exciting writing, opens up difficult subjects to ordinary
people who never would have known about them otherwise.
While the opinion I formed about the Byzantine Empire
would turn out to be less benign than Byron's, *The Station*
sharpened my interest in a subject to which I had been
drawn by the medieval churches in downtown Athens.

Byron combined grimness with a certain hilarity. Here is
his description of the food and sleeping arrangements on
Mount Athos:

Dinner arrived; and with it all the raw hideousness of the
true Athonite meal . . . the grime of cloth and napkins;

spoons, knives and forks slimed with grease . . . those
unmentionable vegetables, resembling large cut nails and
filled with pips tasting of stale pharmaceutical peppermint;
and an omelette of whipped oil. . . . On approaching the
beds, flocks of red bugs might be seen frolicking over the
striped holland of cement mattresses. Fountains of blood—
we wondered whose—squirted from their bodies as we
pressed them flat like gooseberry skins.

Then there are the monks, their lives spent in isolation,
inquiring tenderly after England's political state as though
after "the health of a friend . . . anxious to know if we were
engaged in any war." There is the author's beautiful elegy on
the Trapezuntine Empire, a little piece of Byzantium on the
Black Sea, "negligible in area and void of political achievement," a "minor theme" playing out until 1461, eight years
after the fall of Constantinople. There is his uninhibited comparison, upon entering a Russian monastery, between Greek
and Slavic culture. "The environment was now as Slav as it had
formerly been Greek. The fineness, the delicacy of Hellenism
had given place to something more remote, less coherent.
Flat-nosed Mongols and giant blonds passed by, 'shck' and 'kck'
issuing from their lips in place of the familiar liquids." Strong
opinions everywhere cement the narrative. Byron berates the
expensive American restoration of the Agora in Athens as providing "a pillared playground for cats," while for much less
money many of the icons on Mount Athos might have been
saved. *The Station* radiates the passion of someone discovering
a subject on his own and taking the reader along as he learns.

☙

Mount Athos, because of its legally guaranteed semi-isolation, had probably changed less in the fifty years since Byron wrote *The Station* than almost any place I could have visited that winter. Ouranopolis, the last port on the Athos peninsula at which women are allowed, was in the mid-1970s still a sleepy town of dirt roads and whitewashed two-level houses, with freshly painted green and sky-blue window frames. The cafe and restaurant tables practically sat on the sandy beach, at the end of which was a fortified tower, the color of an olive stone, built by the Byzantine emperor Andronicus II Palaeologus at the turn of the fourteenth century as a look-out against pirates. Bright orange fishing boats rested like flies on the surface of the water. At dawn when the boat, filled with monks and a few tourists, left for Mount Athos, fog was rising off the diaphanous sea like incense smoke from a censer.

Having crossed into the Byzantine domain of the Holy Mountain, the boat passed rambling complexes of monasteries, their walls and roofs lit by the sun in splashy yellow shades. After several hours the boat stopped at the tiny port of Daphni, on the peninsula's southern coast, from where I took a bus up a winding dirt trail to Karyes, the only town on the Holy Mountain. Here Byron had found "an air of activity, almost gaiety," perhaps because he was coming from a monastery in a remoter part of the peninsula. As I had come directly from the outside world, I found Karyes, which means "walnut trees," a place of sleepy silence. It was a Byzantine and Victorian-Gothic concoction of leaden sheeted domes, broken slates, warped wooden planks, sagging roofs, all charming and seemingly on the point of collapse. I remember a raised window that was held up by an empty olive oil jar stuck between it and the sill. The monks, in filthy, hole-ridden black robes and conical hats, were lugging oil jugs, flour sacks, and cooking gas canisters on their shoulders. Their beards were unkempt and many were missing teeth. The old ones made me think of broken tree stumps. They all appeared famished. There was a sign:

GARDEN OF THE VIRGIN MARY, FAR FROM THE SECULAR WORLD. THIS LAND IS SUBJECT TO MIRACLES.

The walk from Karyes to the monastery of Vatopedi, on the peninsula's northern coast, took two and a half hours. I made my way along a trail of late-winter wildflowers. Mount Athos, a snow-streaked triangle, loomed behind me like a giant shadow. Slate-gray boundary walls, massive lime-green trees, olive and cherry groves, and the clang of mule bells heralded Vatopedi, its roofs coated with yellow lichen. It was exactly as described by Byron, "sprouting hosts of tall white chimneys against the blue bay below . . ." Russian onion domes alternated with Italian campaniles. Dickens' Chatsworth seemed utilitarian by comparison.

Fish burbled in deep moats over which bats hovered. I wandered alone through cavernous halls as bare as hospital wards, where here and there I found a magnificent fresco or a little chapel. Dinner, which I took with the monks, was stale bread, lentil and onion gruel, water, and apples. The meal wasn't filling, neither was it as awful as one Byron describes:

cod "salted after it had rotted in the summer sun . . . maca-
roni, embalmed in the juice of goats' udders curdled to a
shrill sourness." The main church was a sulfury subterranean
treasure chest of icons and gold, in whose puddles of darkness sonorous Orthodox chants seemed to be summoning
Persephone back from the Underworld.

The next morning I walked for another two and a half
hours, this time to the Bulgarian monastery of Zographou,
located in the interior of the peninsula between the two
coasts. It was cold and raining hard. My shoes, socks, and
pants below my knees became soaked. Finally, I stumbled
over several bridges and through a gate where, among misty
hills spotted with massive cypress trees and olive groves, a
series of enormous chateaus awaited me. I could not find a
living soul. The entire place appeared deserted. I went into
the church, where my loneliness and discomfort were overcome by awe. The iconostasis, teeming with gold and silver,
half obscured in clouds of sweet incense, reached to the ceiling like the entrance to a pagan temple. A monk with gold
teeth and glazed Slavic features surprised me. His long,
steely-blond hair was tied back with a string. He looked at
my shivering countenance and smiled, inviting me by way of
pantomime to follow him outside, back into the rain, and
then into a building and up several creaking staircases. We
emerged into a small, heated kitchen where a cook stood
with his forearms held up against his chest, his hands dangling like an ape's. He barked orders to another monk with
an imbecilic expression whose clothes were all torn. Soon I
was served a cold meal of spinach gruel and sugared rice with
Turkish coffee.

I looked around at this fantastic mansion with its broken windows and sagging beams. How many occupants were here? I asked in broken Greek. "Six," I was told. Six monks, some of whom appeared only partly sane, to occupy this veritable palace complex!

As I was finishing my lunch, two young men appeared. They were Russian Orthodox seminary students from the United States making a tour of Mount Athos. We fell easily into conversation. I decided to accompany them to the Greek monasteries of Docheiariou and Xenophontos and the Russian monastery of St. Panteleimon, all on the southern coast. The sky cleared as we began to walk. The sunlight dried my pants and shoes. The atmosphere on the southern part of the peninsula was more typically Greek. The monasteries had more whitewash, the vegetation was sparser and less brooding. During our brief stop at Docheiariou, the monks brought us *raki,* Turkish coffee, and water. I never appreciated water until I traveled to Greece: here it is the clear, distilled, metallic, spine-tingling essence of water, a delicacy all its own. At Xenophontos the hospitality was grander still. We were led to a salon with low and fluffy satin couches. Above our heads were icons and pictures of Byzantine emperors and modern Greek monarchs. Again we were brought *raki,* Turkish coffee, and water, along with fruit and sugared candies known as "Turkish delight" (*loukoumia*). The vast dinner hall was lit by a single, dimly lit gas lamp. Through a small window, while finishing my cold lentil soup, I watched the sun set over the water.

My conversation with the two Russian-American seminary students added to the unreality of my strange surroundings. The day had begun with a brutal, lonely rain. Then, in the eerie setting of Zographou, I had met this pair. As we walked the weather cleared, and just as suddenly I was warm, finding friendship and hospitality everywhere. I forgot the names of my two companions, and stupidly did not record much of the conversation in my diary. But the subject of our talk I will never forget.

It was on Mount Athos, more than a quarter of a century ago, that I first heard that the Soviet Union would collapse—and would do so in my lifetime. The two young Russian-Americans spoke to me of the greatness of the czars and of the Russian Orthodox Church, and how both the Romanov dynasty and the Orthodox Church were more legitimate than Leonid Brezhnev's communist regime of the day. A time would come, they assured me, when the czar would again be revered in "Russia," as they called it. I was both fascinated and horrified. Throughout my life, particularly by professors in college, I had been told that the Soviet system, despite its cruelties, was nevertheless an improvement over the reactionary czars. Moreover, because the Cold War had been in progress since before I was born, I unconsciously assumed its permanence. But these seminary students spoke matter-of-factly about the imminent fall of the Soviet Union, as if it would occur next week. I was stunned by their absence of doubt. They provided no analysis, and little explanation. According to them, it was simple: because it was godless, the communist system had no moral legitimacy and, therefore, Russia would be restored to its true self before long.

I attempted to argue with them, but they brushed me

off good-naturedly with a few references to Russia's pre-communist, Orthodox past. I liked them, but I did not believe them. Yet, I believed my surroundings, a time machine that had brought me back to Byzantium: an era when the Eastern Church prevailed with all its passion and intrigues. It was hard here to disagree.

I thought about all this again when, soon afterwards, I discovered Durrell's *Bitter Lemons,* in which he writes of being castigated by a young Israeli journalist: "You English," the journalist says, "seem to . . . be completely under the spell of the Graeco-Roman period, and you judge everything without any reference to Byzantium. Nevertheless, that is where you find the true source of Greek thinking, Greek *moeurs.*" A people's history molds its national character, which reasserts itself during times of change and conflict. Beneath the carapace of communism, Russia, like Greece, was an Eastern Orthodox nation. How would that fact reassert itself?

As the years wore on, with Brezhnev's death in 1982 leading to the infirm, indecisive reigns of Yuri Andropov and Konstantin Chernenko, followed by Mikhail Gorbachev, whose new breed of capitalist-trending authoritarianism toppled, albeit unwittingly, the communist system, the conversation I had had with the two seminary students reverberated louder. Then came the full-fledged return of the Orthodox Church into Russian life, now "Russian" and no longer Soviet, followed by the reburial and consecration of the last czar and czarina as saints.

The professors and political analysts turned out to be wrong, while the two young Russian-Americans I had met on Mount Athos turned out to be right—only because they believed, and believed deeply and morally. History, I learned, is driven not by the smartest people but by those who are the most committed, and those who are the most committed are often not entirely rational. But what they lack in rationality they make up for in passion. Mount Athos was full of passion. The icons I saw there were artistic manifestations of emotion more than of intellect, or of clever analysis.

I remember parting with my two new friends at the Russian monastery of St. Panteleimon, which on the eve of the Russian Revolution had boasted a population of 1,500 monks: in 1913 Rasputin paid a visit. But in the 1970s there were only a dozen monks, pariahs in their native land. Byron's observation in 1928 still rang true. "There is pathos," he writes, "almost tragedy, in this deflation, in this remnant of a once overflowing community debarred from country and traditions—an outpost of old Russia in the Aegean."

Amid the icons, gold-painted Corinthian columns, and candelabra, the twelve monks and the two young Russian-Americans sang loudly and intensely at the morning service, their voices compensating for the hundreds missing from here, and who in spirit would return one day, sooner than I could ever have imagined.

◎◎

From Mount Athos I returned to Athens, from where, after a few days, I headed south to Mistra, that other pole of Byzantium on the Greek mainland.

# ᴥ14ᴥ

## The Morea and Neoplatonism

Leaving Athens in a cheap rental car I first drove south-west toward Corinth. Even in the 1970s, the crummy sprawl seemed only to intensify and I thought that the city would never end. Sex shops and auto parts stores lined what in ancient times was the Sacred Way. Almost half the distance to Corinth the concrete receded finally into a naked, chalky plain, where each green-stubbled, rosy outcrop tore at your heart with its ideographic singularity: so two-dimensional in the thin, wintry air that it was like an abstraction.

The gassy-blue straits of Salamis appeared on my left, crowded with oil tankers: here on one day, September 28, 480 B.C., as many as forty thousand Persian sailors were killed or drowned as the Greek fleet won one of the bloodiest naval battles in history. Before I knew it, I was across the

Corinth Canal—a dizzyingly deep and narrow crevice with ships threading through the sparkling, turquoise bottom. Connecting the Aegean and Ionian seas, the canal separates the Peloponnese from mainland Greece proper. The Peloponnese, the southernmost part of the Balkan peninsula, was known to the medieval Franks and Venetians as the Morea, the word for "mulberry tree," perhaps because they are everywhere in southern Greece. Historians tend to use the word "Peloponnese" when the subject is classical or contemporary history, reserving the term "Morea" for the Byzantine and Ottoman periods.

On the other side of the canal, Acrocorinth rose in distilled, iconic majesty. The natural citadel, two thousand feet high, gave the early inhabitants control of the isthmus, and in the eighth century B.C. a pulsing commercial center grew up around it, sustained by cargo traffic. Corinth, like Athens, Sparta, and Syracuse, became one of the great metropoles and place-names of the ancient world. The founding of Corinthian colonies in Corfu and Sicily made this city-state the dominant mercantile force in western Greece. It was the rise of another maritime power, Athens, in the sixth century B.C.—pitting it against Corinth—that generated many of the crises of Greek politics. The Peloponnesian War began as a struggle between Athens and Corinth over control of Corfu and the Macedonian port of Potidaea, leading Sparta to attack Athens. After the Peloponnesian War was over, the ambitious Corinthians turned against their longtime Spartan allies, vanquishing them in another long struggle known as the Corinthian War. It was only the rise of powers from beyond central Greece—Macedonia and Rome—that ended

Corinthian independence. When the apostle Paul addressed the local Christian community here, Corinth was already a Roman town.

Soon I was off the highway and on a dusty, winding road passing by olive groves, orange trees, and eucalyptuses. By mid-afternoon, in the midst of such languorous beauty, I came upon a dark theater-set of a landscape: an ancient citadel of ugly, Cyclopean rocks in the shadow of two other massive limestone outcrops, where the wind howled and the birds sang as they do before a storm. It was Mycenae, the birthplace of tragedy.

The ancient Greeks, explains the late English scholar F. L. Lucas, were too reasonable to ignore the power of the unreasonable—"too intelligent to become as narrowly intellectual as some minds of the eighteenth-century Enlightenment." To represent this irrational side of the human spirit, the part of us that seethes with destructive passion, the Greeks invented Dionysus: the giver of ecstasy, the god associated with wine and the bestial wildness of the Satyrs, who tore off the limbs of his victims just as his own were torn off by the Titans—before he rose once more from the dead. Dionysus was the god of excess, of losing one's memory in orgiastic eruptions.

From Dionysian unreason comes tragedy: a peculiarly Greek invention founded on the beauty of intolerable truths. "The special characteristic of the Greeks," writes the classicist Edith Hamilton, "was their power to see the world clearly and at the same time as beautiful." That is why realism and romance are the most steady and logical of bedfellows: witness the plays of Euripides, or the novels of Gogol and Conrad, whose baroque characters and landscapes are perfect vehicles to unhappy outcomes. Mycenae chillingly reduces tragedy to its essentials—to the deterministic logic of a mathematical theorem. It strengthens awareness of the forces of passion and irrationality abroad in our world, with its terrorists and other fanatics.

Mycenae dominated Greece during the Bronze Age (1400–1100 B.C.), the Homeric age of heroes. It is the terrible events that befell the House of Atreus here, preserved through the abyss of the millennia thanks to the titanic grandeur of the playwright Aeschylus, that haunt this spot still. Aeschylus, the first writer of tragedy, was a gruff old soldier, on whose tombstone in Gela was written only that he had fought at Marathon. He was near death in 458 B.C. in Gela when he wrote the *Oresteia* trilogy.

The background to this epic begins with Thyestes, the son of Pelops, who has seduced the wife of his brother, Atreus. In revenge, Atreus kills Thyestes' two young sons, cooks their flesh, and serves them to the unknowing Thyestes for dinner. When Thyestes learns what he has eaten he curses the race of Pelops forever. The curse is visited upon Atreus' son, King Agamemnon ("the most resolute"). Agamemnon seals his doom when he decides to sacrifice his daughter Iphigeneia to the goddess Artemis, so that the goddess will send favorable winds for the invasion force that Agamemnon is leading against Troy. In a rage at what her husband has done, Agamemnon's wife, Queen Clytemnestra, takes for a lover Aegisthus, another one of Thyestes' sons, and together they plot to murder Agamemnon on his return from Troy. *Agamemnon,* the first play of the *Oresteia* trilogy, opens at the palace in Mycenae, as the queen is preparing to greet her husband as he nears home.

It was the setting that first got me fixated on this story rather than the other way around: the crazy piles of giant, gray boulders lining the steep path to a monolithic gateway, each stone so large that it seemed a symbol by itself. I gazed uneasily at the two upright lions carved deeply into the stone above the entrance. The "Lion's Gate" was already old at the time Aeschylus lived. As I passed under its crushing immensity, the view narrowed. I saw a crooked stone staircase that led upward to another steeply cobbled path. A pit fell away sharply to my right, exposing a network of walls. The steep grade and the confining ramparts increased the theatrical effect of a carob tree creaking in the wind. In the distance a checkerwork of cultivation ran between sculpted hillsides into the Gulf of Argos. At the top was a series of partitions and the hollow silence of a mountain summit. "The atmosphere of Macbeth's castle and Agamemnon's palace is the same," writes Edith Hamilton. "It is always night there; a heavy murk is in the air; death drifts through the doorways."

From the summit, inside the remains of the palace rooms, you can imagine Clytemnestra staring cynically at the "beacon-light of victory" lit in the plain below, as Agamemnon approaches triumphantly with his troops. You can imagine the oppressive hand of fate as Cassandra warns of the "doom" that the "lustful bitch" Clytemnestra is about to wreak on her husband, while the chorus sings,

> No poured libations can abate . . .
> God's unrelenting hate.

On this bleak terrain, you imagine, too, Agamemnon bleeding to death in his silver bath, as Clytemnestra says,

> . . . from his lips burst forth a gush of blood,
> That splashed me, like a shower of dark red rain;
> And I rejoiced in it, as wheat grows glad
> With heaven's moisture, when the ear is born.

The summit offers a view of the back side of the fortress, where there is another gateway, smaller than the Lion's Gate, but with equal barbaric majesty: the one through which Orestes, the son of Agamemnon and Clytemnestra, escapes after killing his mother in revenge for the murder of his father. This is the subject of *The Libation-Bearers,* the second part of the trilogy, named for Clytemnestra's women servants, whom, in a fit of guilt, she sends to offer propitiatory libations for her dead husband. In this play, Orestes returns to Mycenae after many years abroad to pray at his father's tomb. Here he meets his sister, Electra, and together they swear vengeance against their mother and her lover, both of whom Orestes then slays. Now it is Orestes, rather than Clytemnestra, who is stained with blood defiled by his deed: matricide, an aberration of the laws of nature that will unleash the Furies against him. And thus Orestes flees into exile to northern Greece, where he becomes the founder of Kastoria, a place of leaden skies, the crunch of dead poplar leaves, and mountains grooved with snow.

In *The Eumenides* ("The Kind Goddesses"), the last part of the trilogy, Orestes travels from Kastoria to Apollo's shrine at Delphi to hide from the Furies—crones with snakes for hair who torment the young for crimes committed against their elders. The Delphic Oracle commands Orestes to go to Athens to stand trial for his mother's murder. There he is acquitted and the Furies are persuaded to remain in Athens and reign as "the kind goddesses." Thus, the justice of the state prevails and the cycle of violence is ended. But it is fear that helps undergird such justice. As Robert Graves tells us, the Greeks used the term "the kind goddesses" because they were afraid to mention the Furies by name in conversation.

Walking down the hillside, I saw other tourists sitting alone or in small quiet groups, oblivious to the bad weather, a guidebook or copies of Homer and Aeschylus in hand, the dark beauty of the scene the perfect backdrop for the playwright's exacting analysis of human nature.

୧୬

Later that day I reached Nauplion. Failing sunlight flooded the grid of narrow streets. Church bells pealed: a fast and gentle cascade of rings rather than the measured gong-gong of the West. I ate a simple dinner of fried squid and feta cheese by the harbor. Through the restaurant window the water of dusk faded to murky bronze as a small oil tanker passed by. Because it figures little in classical history, I simply enjoyed Nauplion as a perfect spot. Nauplion, fought over by the Venetians and the Turks, rose to prominence only in 1829, when it became the first capital of modern Greece before the seat of government was moved to Athens in 1834. That lone fact stirred my interest.

The Peloponnese had been the principal battleground for the Greek War of Independence against the Ottoman

Empire: as much a clear-cut struggle of good versus evil as an anarchic Balkan bloodletting that demonstrates how, as always, the weakening and collapse of empires is messy business. The uprising against the Turks was led by clerics and brigands known as klephts. After the Greeks captured Tripolis in the central Peloponnese, they massacred twelve thousand Turkish civilians. The Turks responded by killing more than twice as many Greeks on the island of Chios, near the coast of Asia Minor. Though western statesmen feared a power vacuum in the eastern Mediterranean, Greek independence became a fashionable cause among the early-nineteenth-century intellectual elite of Europe, of whom the most notable figure was the poet Lord Byron (a distant relation of the early-twentieth-century travel writer Robert Byron). Byron sailed to Greece, where he died of fever at Messolonghi while trying to unite the forces of the various klephtic chieftains, whose intrigues and rivalries almost defy analysis. The tide turned in the klephts' favor when in October 1827 there was a collision between the British, French, and Russian navy squadrons and the Ottoman fleet in the Bay of Navarino in the southwestern Peloponnese that ended in the almost total destruction of the Ottomans. But even after Greece obtained its independence from the Sultan in 1829, factional struggles went on. The klephts from the Mani, in the extreme south of the Peloponnese, remained a law unto themselves. In 1831, outside of a church in Nauplion, the Maniots assassinated John Capodistria, modern Greece's first president. The disorganized struggle of the Greek klephts against the Ottoman Empire in the 1820s would give me a point of comparison when, in the 1980s, I reported on the similarly disorganized struggle of the Afghan *mujahidin* against the Soviet Union.

☙❧

Rounding the Gulf of Argos, I ascended into the higher elevations of the central Peloponnese. It was among the loneliest and most rugged landscapes I would ever see: ranks of moss-bearded, dinosauric humps advancing in dreary majesty to the horizon. Hairpin turns were marked by makeshift votive stands: rusted boxes of iron and glass topped by a cross, with an icon and half-burnt candle inside, marking the spot where a traffic accident was avoided, or was fatal. Then came a gaunt tableland and another nest of icy spires, the mountains of Arcadia, where I turned south toward the vale of Sparta.

I passed the village of Mantinea, its tiled roofs hugging the sides of a mountain. In the Peloponnesian War, Mantinea dominated a mini-alliance of surrounding city-states that allied itself with Argos and Corinth to resist being engulfed by nearby Sparta. Passing through rolling fields of flowering judases, the Parnon range rose to my left. To my right, to the southwest just before I reached Sparta, the saw-tooth ramparts of the Taygetus rose sheer under a grim cloud mantle to a height of seven thousand feet. The sea with its soft, grape-colored hills by Nauplion seemed a vague memory now: ancient Sparta was a land power, not a maritime one like Athens. Mulberry trees and silvery olive leaves glittering in the wind heralded the Spartan plain. At last I was near my destination.

❧

Save for the works of Thucydides, Xenophon, and others, Sparta is lost to antiquity, its archaeological remains paltry and the modern town a disappointing gridwork of concrete. But three miles to the west of Sparta, beyond the meandering Eurotas River, lies the embodiment of Greek landscape enjoyments, as well as the remnants of the final phase of classical civilization in any form.

When Hadrian rebuilt the Pantheon, it was partly because the Roman Empire was in danger of fragmenting and different people were worshiping different gods, so he built a house of unity for all the gods of the peoples of the empire. Unfortunately, his plan didn't work, and Christianity, whose inverse purpose was to unite the empire under a single god, swept into the fray. Constantine the Great, the first Christian emperor of Rome, moved the center of imperial power east to the Bosphorus, where "Rome in the East," renamed Constantinople, was the capital of the Eastern Roman, or Byzantine, Empire for a thousand years. And it was on a spur of the Taygetus called Mistra, at the edge of the Eurotas valley, where Byzantium was to finally expire. In Mistra, because of political unrest in Constantinople, the Serbo-Greek Constantine XI Dragases was crowned in 1449—last of the eighty-eight emperors of Byzantium and last heir to Caesar Augustus in Rome.

Seventeenth-century travelers were so overwhelmed by Mistra's beauty that they confused it with the remains of Sparta itself, so as to invest that mighty city-state with a demonstrable aura of romance. It was Chateaubriand, passing through in 1806 en route from Paris to Jerusalem, who was the first of the moderns to realize that Mistra and Sparta were two different places. Robert Byron came with his companions in 1927 to photograph the frescoes in the churches, to prove that Mistra and what it represented were more important to the West than Sparta. Inspired by the daily treks he made to Mistra from the modern town of Sparta, Byron, in *The Station,* writes some of his most moving lines.

> For those epicures in landscape who demand not only form but colour, for whom central Europe is but a chromatic photograph and an Alp in a sunset comparable only to the asbestos in a gas-stove, the Levant is without peer. And in all the Levant . . . there is no place where the divine soul of the earth can so fill the heart, so suffocate the eyes with tears . . . as the Eurotas valley. Last year, as this, we had come every morning from Sparta. And at the end of each day we had plodded home along the dusty road through the olive groves, bidding the peasants good evening and good night. Never in life will the memory of those May nights escape; of the air enveloping, dark and real, the breathing human kiss of the earth. . . .

In 1948, rather than read Aeschylus in Mycenae, or another classical writer *in situ,* a young Anglo-American traveler and World War II veteran, Kevin Andrews, found himself a nearby terrace under a plane tree where, in sight of this last living vestige of Byzantium, he spent a week reading several Byzantine histories and a long verse chronicle written in fourteenth-century Romaic (similar to modern-day Greek). Andrews' book *The Flight of Ikaros: Travels in*

*Greece During a Civil War* was written a generation after Byron's. Yet it seems older, because the Greece that Andrews experienced was poorer and war ravaged. In the mid-1980s, I would visit Andrews at his flat in Athens. He wore the black sheepskin of a Greek peasant inside his unheated, wintry quarters, surrounded by the musty odor of sea shells which he had collected and the naive jewelry he had made by hand. On his desk was a pile of rejection slips. When I entered his flat he had been reading a twenty-year-old review of one of his guidebooks of Greece. "Myconos," he told me, "I haven't been back since 1947. I wouldn't touch it with a ten-foot pole." Around him was a sprawling, polluted city that bore scant resemblance to the one he had fallen in love with in the 1940s. "My father was English, my mother American, and I was born in China, so I never had any roots. Greece is as much my home as anywhere." Though his real father was the British solider St. John "Chips" Smallwood, Andrews was also the step-son of Roy Chapman Andrews, who in the 1920s led several expeditions into the Gobi Desert for the American Museum of Natural History in New York, making him the prototype for the fictional Indiana Jones. Married at one time to Nancy Cummings, the daughter of the poet E. E. Cummings, Kevin Andrews at the time I met him had no family, and drowned in 1989. In addition to *The Flight of Ikaros,* his youthful travels also resulted in his superb *Castles of the Morea.* While I admired him for his writing, like the two old painters I had met in Syracuse, I was afraid of ending up like him. Mistra's beauty—and that of a handful of other places—had obsessed him for so long that he seemed to have done little more the rest of his life than look back on it.

The first time I came to Mistra it was damp and cold, with a fine, cleansing mist. The most beautiful landscapes are the subtlest, they drain you rather than overwhelm you. I walked up the stone steps of the medieval city's main gate, where I could see the valley through which I had come. Sparta lay in the middle distance, its concrete sprawl barely noticeable among the masses of olive trees that stretched to the foothills of Parnon in the east. Mulberries, judases, the occasional cypress, ripe orange and lemon trees, and oleanders that had yet to bud further distinguished a tapestry of cultivation anchored on broad contours of rich red earth. The beauty of the Eurotas valley is a consequence of delicate shadows and disparate brown and lime-green shades, as if the earth were arrested in late autumn. Here is the original heart of Greece, where Helen reigned with her husband Menelaus before she and her lover Paris absconded to Troy, centuries before the founding of Athens.

A racket of clicking leaves spiced the air. Upon this snowy fang of the Taygetus, medieval ramparts rose up around me like minimalist sculptures. Thyme, milkweed, basil, and sage lay alongside golden broom and spurge and wildflowers that were like a splattering of bright paint. On the serpentine path that led up into this sarcophagus of a medieval city the cobblestone grooves were crammed with fallen bright pink petals. But it was the walls of Mistra, rising a thousand feet off the valley floor, that were the most humbling element in the landscape. All over the Mediterranean that winter I had been captivated by old walls. Here, their decayed beauty seemed to reach an apogee: ruined belfries and cracked shells of churches adorned with intricate brick festoons—a Karnak or Pompeii of the late Byzantine era. For millennia artists have tried to replicate the beauty of nature. Here brickworkers and stoneworkers had almost outdone her.

The frescoes in Mistra's cold and badly illuminated churches comprise a vision of statuesque saints floating down to shadowy sea depths: in their fine robes and aristocratic poses, they could also be the great philosophers and dramatists of ancient Athens, weightless against a background of riotous colors. In Mistra you experience pagan antiquity and medieval Orthodoxy as part of the same Hellenism. Because the Greeks through the Eastern Empire culturally replaced Rome from within, here are the stylistic successors of the Roman and early Byzantine mosaics that I had seen in Sousse and Piazza Armerina. "Western Christs expose their wounds; Eastern Christs sit enthroned in ungesticulating splendour," writes Patrick Leigh Fermor, who could have been describing some of Mistra's frescoes in which the Virgin Mary wears the demeanor of an aloof oriental empress. Upon visiting Mistra, Robert Byron after World War I, Kevin Andrews and Patrick Leigh Fermor after World War II, and the historians Steven Runciman and C. M. Woodhouse later on, all developed an intense interest about its past. Even when historians write dryly, it is often the beauty and aesthetics of a place that have inspired their work.

༼༽

Mistra's emergence as the great Byzantine metropolis of the Morea was largely the result of the anarchy that followed the end of classical Greek civilization. When the Romans came to the Peloponnese in 146 B.C. they sacked the fortress in

Corinth. Later the entire Peloponnese would be open to waves of Visigoths, Avars, Huns, Bulgars, and Slavs. In the sixth century A.D., the emperor Justinian refortified Corinth, but the invasions continued, particularly those of the Slavs, who filtered into the hills of the southern Morea around Sparta, known since antiquity as Lacedaemon. Then in the early thirteenth century, in the wake of the Crusader conquest of Constantinople, the knights of the Fourth Crusade divided up parts of the Byzantine Empire, allowing Franks and Burgundians to march in their hundreds into the Morea. In 1249, one of the Franks, Guillaume de Villehardouin, built Mistra's impenetrable hilltop stronghold in order to protect the vale of Sparta from the Slav Milengi tribe hiding in the nearby valleys of the Taygetus. But a decade later the tide turned against the Latin knights. Because of the defeat of the Crusaders in Macedonia and northwestern Asia Minor, in addition to the recapture of Constantinople and the arrest of Guillaume himself, Guillaume was obliged to buy back his freedom by ceding the strongholds of Mistra and Monemvasia to the Greeks. Even so, Mistra might soon have been retaken for western Christendom by the French Angevins had not the Revolt of the Sicilian Vespers in 1282 undermined Angevin imperial ambitions in Constantinople and the southern Morea. But thanks to events in Sicily, Byzantine power subsequently stabilized here. Further incursions by the Franks were prevented. And in 1348 Constantinople raised Mistra to the status of a despotate.

It was only here in the Morea that the Greeks were able to revive politically and culturally, even as Thrace and Macedonia were being ravaged by Serbs and Bulgars, and economic control of Constantinople had been wrested by the Italian city-states. For over a hundred years, until 1460, when the last despot of Mistra, Dimitrios, surrendered to the Ottoman Turks (seven years after the final fall of Constantinople, and a year before the fall of Greek Trebizond on the Black Sea), Mistra enjoyed a renaissance in the arts and humanities, attracting thinkers from throughout Byzantium, while the rest of the Byzantine Empire petrified. "In this airy casket of a city," Fermor writes,

> a succession of purple-born princes reigned: strange and stately figures in their fur-trimmed robes and melon-crowned caps-of-maintenance. The libraries filled with books, poets measured out their stanzas, and on the scaffolding of one newly-risen church after another painters mixed their gypsum and cinnabar and egg-yolk and powdered crocus and zinc and plotted the fall of drapery and described the circumference of haloes.

Mistra boasted twenty thousand inhabitants and sprawling suburbs. A haven from siege, plague, and civil unrest, it attracted minorities of Jews, Spaniards, Venetians, and Florentines. In the first half of the fifteenth century, Mistra was the most prestigious address in the Byzantine Empire, after Salonika and Constantinople itself. Near the top of the hill here, the vast and rambling Palace of the Despots makes Mistra's enormity suddenly obvious: so much so that during Turkish rule, until the visit of Chateaubriand, the ruins were identified with the ancient Palace of Menelaus.

❦

The obsession I developed about Mistra led to a similar obsession with its most important and legendary figure, the Neoplatonist philosopher Georgios Gemistos Plethon, a kindler of the Italian Renaissance. Relatively little is known about Gemistos except for an extended visit he made to Florence late in life, in 1439, when he made a great impression on the Italian elite, principally on Cosimo de' Medici, with his lecture "On the Differences of Aristotle from Plato." The British historian C. M. Woodhouse considers Gemistos the ultimate transitional figure: "the last of the Hellenes" because of his emphasis on classical antiquity, and "the first of the Greeks, in the sense of modern nationalists," because he employed pagan ideals in a quest to revitalize Hellenism.

Gemistos was born to a scholarly family in Constantinople. No one is sure of the exact year of his birth, though it is generally agreed to have been sometime in the late 1350s or early 1360s. Like many he studied Christian theology, from which philosophy had yet to wrest itself. But under Jewish teachers he also studied Jewish, Persian, and ancient Greek religions. His interest in Plato grew to the point at which he became too controversial for the Orthodox clergy in the Byzantine capital, and sometime after the turn of the fifteenth century he relocated to the more liberal environment of Mistra. There he would spend the rest of his life, except for the one trip to Italy. About the time he moved to Mistra he changed his name to Plethon, which, like Gemistos, means "full," but which also sounded like "Plato." He lived to be more than ninety, dying in Mistra in 1452, the year before the Ottoman Turks conquered Constantinople.

Plethon lived his life against the background of a dying Byzantine Empire—of an entire civilization in decay. Yet he understood, in the words of Steven Runciman, that the "one great asset" Byzantium possessed was that it "had preserved unadulterated the learning and literature of ancient Greece," to the envy of the scholars of the West. Pagan ideals and practices had never completely disappeared from Greek life. The emperor Julian the Apostate had briefly resurrected paganism in the fourth century, and elements of it still survived among both urban intellectuals and rural peasants. Plethon's use of paganism to foment a Greek national resurgence, in the face of a political and religious onslaught from the Latin West that was leaving Greece exposed to military pressure from the Ottoman Empire, would have the most unintended of consequences.

Byzantium's political failure, Plethon knew, was the result of a spiritual failure, since any state not anchored in sound moral principles must falter sooner or later. According to the late British scholar Philip Sherrard, Plethon believed that this spiritual failure rested on two elements: the "arbitrariness" of God's divine action, so that rationality played no part in the Greek Christian faith, a fact which undermined the political culture; and the blind rejection of polytheism that had "eliminated all notion of an intermediary intellectual world"—the world of ideas—leaving only the absolutism of God the creator. In making these claims, Plethon was picking up a strand of ideas left untouched since St. Augustine, who, a millennium earlier in North Africa, had posited that because the soul is separate from the body, the physical world needed to be studied in its own right: this provided the religious justification for rationalism and science. Reason could exist outside Christianity (or any other monotheistic religion) and still be moral so long as it was grounded in universal principles. Thus, the rebirth of Greece in the fifteenth century would depend upon an intellectual order that was compatible with, but separate from, the Orthodox Church. This fact is relevant today not only in the Orthodox world, but in the Islamic one, too, where religion has degenerated into an austere ideology, stifling independent thought.

In his lifetime, Plethon's bitterest opponents were the Aristotelians. As Philip Sherrard explains in *The Greek East and the Latin West,* the fact that Aristotle had already been assimilated into the "universal Christian consciousness" rendered him somewhat neutralized, and thus more acceptable by the standards of the age; whereas Plato's beliefs lay outside the Orthodox establishment, making him in a sense the more "pagan" of the two ancient philosophers. The dispute between the Neoplatonists and the Aristotelians obsessed generations of intellectuals, though much of it remains obscure to us. Sometimes it had less to do with Plato and Aristotle as they actually were in antiquity than with what they came to represent by the time of the Renaissance. Supporters of Aristotle like George Trapezuntius (a Cretan whose parents were from Trebizond) wilfully distorted Plethon's writings, so that many believed Plethon sought to replace Christian Orthodoxy with paganism, rather than restore Christianity by adopting certain aspects of pagan thought.

Still, by our own standards, Plethon appears more reactionary than his rival Trapezuntius: for his hero Plato places less emphasis on the individual than on some higher, ahistorical, and utopian order; whereas Aristotle, because he believed that man was limited to his own observations of the world around him, deduced that man's supreme purpose was his human destiny within the life of the *polis.* Neoplatonists like Plethon wanted to strengthen the Greek *ethnos* through a mystical order above that of the individual, while Aristotelians seemed more oriented toward individual rights within a cosmopolitan society.

The outcome of the debate was opposite to what both groups had intended. Though the debate was never resolved, it played a significant role in the rediscovery of classical Greek thought in general, which ultimately found fruition in the works of Machiavelli and other Renaissance thinkers. Rather than revitalize the Orthodox Church through paganism, Plethon was part of a process that demolished the medieval notion of "Christendom" altogether, replacing it with science and secular politics. Moreover Plethon, during his visit to Italy, introduced an acquaintance, Paolo Toscanelli, to Strabo's *Geographica,* which unlike the works of Ptolemy was unknown in the West. And it was Toscanelli who brought Strabo to the attention of Christopher Columbus.

Some of the most beautiful of the frescoes at Mistra were executed in the same period that Plethon lived and taught—a last burst of creativity before the entire scene went black. In 1460 the last despot ceded Mistra to the Turks. Mistra was to change hands back and forth between the Turks and Venetians before being burnt by the Russians and again by the Albanians in the late eighteenth century, and by the Turks once more in the early nineteenth. Yet what is left is more than enough.

❦

From Sparta I followed a descending valley south to the Laconic Gulf. After several days inland, the port of Gytheion lured me with its long line of outdoor restaurants and gleaming balustrades. A waiter came with a giant paper napkin and placed it completely over my square table, anchoring it with plastic clips against the wind. Then he filled the table with seafood appetizers and a can of white wine. Veiny brush strokes of mountains appeared across the water: in Greece you are rarely beyond sight of the next landfall.

My memory of sea-washed Gytheion is mixed up with memories of the Aegean islands I visited over the years. I went there usually in late March and April, and these islands are associated in my mind with Pascha, Orthodox Easter, a bigger holiday than its Latin equivalent, where Christians join their pagan ancestors to release the world from the barrenness and darkness of winter.

On Syros, I remember a church packed to the walls with people chanting the exultant story of the Resurrection, which culminates with the visit of the three women to the tomb of Joseph of Arimathea. When the clock struck twelve the priest, quietly proclaiming *"Christos anesti"* ("Christ has risen"), lit a lone candle with which he then lit someone else's, who then lit another's, as each person proclaimed *"Christos anesti"* to the person next to him, until all of our candles were lit and the darkness inside the church had been defeated. Shouting in unison *"Christos anesti,"* we threw open the church doors to hear palm trees singing in the nighttime breeze, and lit the candles of the crowd waiting on the steps outside.

On Samos, near the Turkish shore, soldiers waited in formation in the cold night until the chanting grew louder inside the church and the doors burst open, revealing a forest of lit candles. Then the band struck up and the soldiers led a procession of clergy holding crosses and icons, as little boys scampered through the crowd firing cap guns. Having reached the square, the crowd lifted their candles, icons, and crosses to the night sky in a gesture at once pitiable and defiant.

On Chios, the morning after Easter, I walked through the garden of an abandoned house, noisy with bees and overgrown with lilacs, jasmine, and lemon blossoms. Holding a huge key, a Greek friend whose grandmother had grown up in the house opened the corroded wooden door. Inside, the plaster was peeling off the walls, revealing the original stones of the house beneath. My face itched from the dust and cobwebs. Then we climbed to an upper floor whose windows offered a view of the low hills of Cesme on the Turkish coast. On the floor I noticed a wooden trunk, which I pried open. Inside were doilies, old photos, and a solitary, painted egg. I held the egg in my hand but was afraid to crack it. There was something frightening about this egg that had been in a trunk for decades. So I put it back inside the trunk: a part of the past that should remain private.

## THE LAST PASHA OF THE

## MEDITERRANEAN

Beyond Gytheion stretches a savage and narrowing prong of the Taygetus that forms the southernmost peninsula of the Peloponnese: the Mani. Here is arguably the remotest part of Greece, home of blood feuds and the fiercest of the klephts. The Maniots were the last of the Greeks to be converted to Christianity, abandoning paganism only toward the end of the ninth century. Walled villages with medieval towers look out over vast and empty limestone headlands that drop off in mid-air to foaming bays below. It is a landscape that intimates the gaunt loneliness of Libya directly to the south.

I returned to the Mani for the first time in several decades in March 2002. From Gytheion I drove southwest across the peninsula, through a break in the mountains, until I reached the other shore. Each bay, as I wound my way north along the coast, was more spectacular than the next. A sprinkle of signs indicated only a mild rash of tourist development. Otherwise, there was just the sleepy silence of stony fields buzzing with insects and the distant thud of waves. Kardamyli, a huddle of stone houses with faded roof tiles, flaunts its perfect synthesis of classical and medieval landscapes. The town faces a monumental slab of sea, the romantic shorthand of Homeric Greece, where far out over the horizon King Nestor, a sage presence in both the *Iliad* and the *Odyssey,* entertained Odysseus' son Telemachus at his palace in Pylos; while to its rear is a dark and angry pile of the Taygetus, a testament to the rugged depths of the interior with its obscure tribal and ethnic struggles that extended from the close of antiquity through the nineteenth-century Greek War of Independence.

Entering Kardamyli from the south, the land trips down toward the sea in terraced fields of olives and young cypresses, where a villa with red roof tiles and its own little bay gives onto the Messinian Gulf: the setting for a flawless Mediterranean existence. Because the Mediterranean has no tides, "it has few desolate aspects," notes Stendhal. "These shores are never spoiled by that half-league of sand and mud which . . . sadden the traveler and show him boats leaning dejectedly on their sides." I turned down a winding dirt track and made my way to the villa.

I spotted an old and battered white Peugeot and pulled over beside it. A massive door appeared through the thickets of a long stone wall. Opening it, I noticed a stack of olive wood logs, several walking sticks, and high rubber boots. A young Greek woman came and told me to follow her to

"Kyrie Michali." "Mr. Michael?" I wondered, unsure if I had come to the right house. But she led the way through a loggia, where I felt the wind move the sea like a flutter of draperies. We came to another heavy door, which this time she pushed open.

I fell into a long, enormous library, smoky and pungent from the olive wood burning in the chimney and an old kerosene heater. Battered old bindings lay in recessed shelves piled to the ceiling. The floor was covered in oriental and sheepskin rugs. Between the rows of book shelves, arched windows gave a prospect of the gnarled and silvery olive groves that spread out below. Close to the door was a sitting area of low, Turkish-style couches with brocaded pillows, above which the Mediterranean, the color of ink and steel in the late winter sunlight, appeared through a white-washed portcullis. Amid such magnificence, a man with thick, curly white hair and a face lined with the crevices of age appeared out of the woodsmoke, like some old pasha in a serai, and extended his hand with a great smile.

His clothes reeked of burnt logs. A fine white-collared shirt beneath two tattered mud-colored sweaters was the only indication that he was not penniless. The walking sticks I had seen, the layers of sweaters, and the ruddy complexion spoke of a healthy life lived in chilly rooms.

"She referred to you as Kyrie Michali?" I asked, confused.

"Oh, yes. If you say 'Patrick' here, they call you 'Petros,' who is a fine old saint but not suited to me. I say, it's time we had a drink. Shall it be *ouzo*?"

By the entrance to the library, stuffed with pillows,

books, and paintings, and yet spare and sparkling with the light, stood a counter crowded with spirits. We each had a sip of *ouzo* and he led me to a table near the sitting area where a lunch had been prepared: *phasolia* (white haricot beans), boiled eggs sprinkled with pepper, goat cheese, salad, and a decanted liter of *retsina,* homemade from a nearby village. "Come now, forge on," he said, encouraging me to eat and drink.

The voice that had greeted me, and had earlier given me directions over the phone, was ripe with a vibrant regality and a demonstrable lust for existence. It was a mellifluous voice belonging to another era: a voice that might have been coming through the static of World War II radio waves.

෨෧

At the age of eighteen, in December 1933, Patrick Leigh Fermor quit the Royal Military Academy at Sandhurst and set off on foot for Constantinople. The rucksack he carried was the one that had accompanied Robert Byron, David Talbot Rice, and Mark Ogilvie-Grant on their trip to Mount Athos six years earlier. Fermor walked from Holland through Hitler's Germany and on to Austria across the Great Hungarian Plain and the Balkans, living on a pound a week and sleeping one night in a castle, the next in a barn. Having reached Constantinople, he wandered over to Greece, spending his twentieth birthday at the Russian monastery of St. Panteleimon on Mount Athos. Later, he spent two years in a country house with a magnificent library in northern Romania, the equivalent of a university education. On the outbreak of World War II, he became a British liaison officer with the Greek army fighting Mussolini's forces in Albania. Following the Nazi occupation of Crete, he infiltrated the island to help organize the resistance, living in the mountains disguised as a Cretan shepherd in a black turban and sash and armed with a silver-and-ivory dagger. With several other Englishmen he organized and carried out the 1944 kidnapping of General Werner Kreipe, Nazi commander of the Sevastopol Division in Crete, whom Fermor's group forced-marched to the sea, where a boat awaited them in darkness for the escape to Egypt. The kidnapping was the subject of a book, *Ill Met by Moonlight* by W. Stanley Moss, Fermor's comrade in the affair, and a British movie of the same title, with Dirk Bogarde playing Fermor. Though the Germans put a price on his head, Fermor returned to occupied Crete, "my island home where the minotaurs roam," as he wrote romantically in a letter. He was later awarded the DSO (Distinguished Service Order) and the OBE (Order of the British Empire).

With World War II over, Fermor went to the Caribbean, about which he wrote a travel book and then a novel, *The Violins of Saint-Jacques,* later to become an opera. His permanent return to Greece in the early 1950s would result in his greatest works. *Mani* and *Roumeli,* about separate regions in Greece, represent arguably the high-water marks of literary travel writing in English: two books that are as delightfully humorous as Robert Byron's *The Station,* but with smoother narratives, more stunning phraseology, and wider-ranging erudition, if that is possible.

In *Mani* we see dolphins as "beautiful abstractions of speed," learn that the coals in Greek water pipes burn through "the *toumbeki* leaves from Ispahan," and that the taste of *retsina* may have its origin in antiquity, with "the custom of caulking the leaks in barrels and wine skins with lumps of resin." In one memorable passage, the author relates a dinner with a friend in nearby Kalamata, on a day so hot that the stones of the embankment "flung back the heat like a casserole with the lid off." On an impulse, Fermor and his friend carry their iron table and chairs a few yards out so that they can sit waist deep in the water, with the table seeming to levitate a few inches above it. The Greek waiter, with a "quickly-masked flicker of pleasure," then steps unhesitatingly into the sea "with a butler's gravity" and delivers their grilled mullet, which the two dip by the tails for a second into the water "to enjoy their marine flavour to the utmost."

In *Roumeli,* Fermor writes about a region in central Greece not to be found on modern maps. Here we are treated to disquisitions on eastern monasticism, on the dying dialect of the paganistic Sarakatsan tribe and the secret language of the Kravara, and the more than sixty characteristics and symbols that distinguish the western Hellene mentality from the eastern Romios one. Among other feats of virtuosity, the author retraces the steps of Lord Byron in the Pindus mountains, and provides seven pages on the sounds of the Greek world:

> Arcadia is the double flute, Arachova the jingle of hammers
> on the strings of a dulcimer, Roumeli a klephtic song heck-
> led by dogs and shrill whistles, Epirus the trample of ele-
> phants, the Pyrrhic stamp, the heel slapped in the Tsamiko

dance, the sign of Dodonian holm-oaks and Acroceraunian thunder and rain. . . .

In 1977, Fermor published the first volume of his memoir about walking through Europe as a youth, *A Time of Gifts: On Foot to Constantinople; From the Hook of Holland to the Middle Danube,* a never-to-be-equaled masterpiece in which the excitement of new landscapes, frightening politics, and strange civilizations explode before a hungry young mind. In one scene he describes an inn that has just filled with singing Nazi brown-shirts: "Beer, caraway seed, beeswax, pine-logs and melting snow combined with the smoke of thick, short cigars in a benign aroma across which every so often the ghost of sauerkraut would float." The charm of the scene, the dreamy songs of love under linden trees, and the bespectacled faces of some of the brown-shirts, who "might have been clerks or students," make it hard for the young traveler "to connect the singers with organized bullying and the smashing of Jewish shop windows . . ." Everywhere he is showered with presents. After losing his diary, a German baron, feeling sorry for him, gives him a volume of Horace "beautifully printed on thin paper in Amsterdam in the middle of the seventeenth century, bound in hard green leather with gilt lettering."

Nine years later came the second volume, *Between the Woods and the Water: On Foot to Constantinople; From the Middle Danube to the Iron Gates,* which features a close-up portrait of a Transylvanian culture that would soon be destroyed by Nazism and communism, as the author sojourns with some of the last of the great Hungarian landowning families, with their feudal manners, vast libraries, and midnight bonfires.

Now at the age of eighty-seven, Fermor had been struggling for sixteen years in Kardamyli with the third and final volume of the memoir, which would take him from the Iron Gates of the Danube (where the borders of Romania, Yugoslavia, and Bulgaria meet) to Constantinople.

☙❧

"Tell me about your background," he said as we enjoyed the homemade *retsina,* the finest and most delicate I ever had.

Talking loud on account of his bad hearing, I gave him the story of my life in about four sentences: I had grown up in a working-class area of New York City, had gone to a non-prestigious college, had visited rural Greece while young, and realized that Greece—and books like his own, which I found out about because of Greece—somehow provided me with a direction in journalism that I followed thereafter. When I mentioned that I was writing about the Mediterranean in the off-season, he said:

"I lived in Hydra for two winters. The locals only accept you after you've been through a winter. After that they think of you as autochthonous." It emerged that while the directions he had given me to the house were not wholly correct, and while he had forgotten several times that I had driven rather than hiked here, his vocabulary was still profuse and at the ready. Quoting Evelyn Waugh, he reminded me that good writing requires three elements: "euphony, clarity, and concision."

We exchanged reminiscences separated by forty-five years about the Russian monastery of St. Panteleimon. "Yes, the Cold War did seem interminable back when you met those two Russian seminarians. You know," he went on, "it was because of Byron's book that I made up my mind to go to Mount Athos after reaching Constantinople. I met Byron later on. I was knocking about London before World War II. It was at a jazz club. He was rather tight, but delightful, always engaging in intellectual arguments. He was of the *Brideshead* generation. Ah, it was a shame he was lost at sea." Robert Byron was drowned in 1941 at the age of thirty-six, when the Germans torpedoed the ship that was taking him to Cairo to be a war correspondent. "Of course, had he lived he would have thrown himself into the Greek resistance struggle against the Germans. The causes he would have gotten involved in! He was so, so abundant.

"Though, no one was as abundant as Larry," going on, referring to Durrell. "Larry I knew quite well. He was infectious, vibrant, an eruption of life. He was a very short man, yet so full of compacted energy. He could swim faster than anyone I knew—a feat for a little man. He could play any string instrument, sing too. He got tight a lot, in a good way I mean. His conversation was sparkling, immense. The sentences just flew out of his mouth, complex, fully formed and grammatical. It was extraordinary. Cyprus shattered him, though. At first he couldn't accept that the Cypriots could hate the English the way they did, that their interests were different from ours. Maybe that's why he could write perceptively about the upheaval there. Politics always intrudes."

We spoke about the Middle East, the shuttle diplomacy of the 1970s, and the Israeli-Palestinian nightmare. I deliberately mentioned Freya Stark, the British diplomat and travel writer. A smile broke out along the gorges of his face. "Yes," he said, standing up, looking out the portcullised window at the sea, "her voice would move from register to register, up and down," waving his hand like a conductor, "funny, then terribly quiet, always getting her way with generals and viceroys. She came here once or twice. No, two or three times I think it was."

He hadn't known about the new biography of Stark by Jane Fletcher Geniesse; nor was he aware that former king Simeon of Bulgaria had been elected prime minister there, even though the last volume of his memoir would deal with that country. Of course, none of that mattered in regards to what he was specifically writing about. But when I mentioned Gemistos Plethon, I was regaled with a low-voiced disquisition, barely rising above a mumble, of how Plethon's remains were exhumed in 1465, thirteen years after his death, when Sigismondo Malatesta, the ancestral ruler of Rimini and mercenary commander of a Venetian expeditionary force, held the lower town of Mistra and refused to withdraw ahead of a Turkish army without first claiming the body of his favorite philosopher. Malatesta, a discriminating patron of the arts and philosophy, reburied Plethon in a sarcophagus in an outer wall of his Tempio Malestiano in Rimini. Here in full force was the erudition that flavors every page of Fermor's books: the unearthing from expert sources of what is so worthwhile to know, but which so few of us do know.

"You can't be a travel writer," he said. "You can only be a

writer who needs to travel in order to further your inquiries. Now, you must read the new edition of *Ill Met by Moonlight* to find out what happened in Crete in 1944, and I must read the new biography of Freya Stark."

"I'll have my assistant send it to you," I said, explaining, somewhat apologetically, that being close to fifty, I had decided that I finally needed an assistant or I would simply get overwhelmed.

"God, I've never had an assistant. But I suppose it's all right as long as you continue to do your own research. The whole point of writing is to learn through your inquiries and then pass it on to others. What's the point of being a writer if someone else is doing it for you?"

The Greek woman arrived with cups of Greek coffee on a brass tray. I glanced up from the rainbow bubbles in the coffee to some of the book shelves: the eight-volume *Frankish History of Italy, Leake's Travels in Northern Greece, Gordon's History of the Greek Revolution,* a rebound eleventh edition of the *Encyclopaedia Britannica* published in 1910—"the last good one," Fermor noted. "You should always have good reference works in the room where you dine. The best sorts of arguments start over dinner, and you must have the means available to settle them."

"Those pictures?" I asked, pointing to two modern paintings hung above the liquor tray.

"Ghika, the Picasso of Greece. He gave them to me."

Nikos Hadjikyriakos Ghika was the most important Greek painter of the twentieth century. By adapting cubism to the Greek landscape, with its white geometric shapes and winding, cobblestone streets, Ghika refined Picasso's vision.

Ghika, who was a friend of Wassily Kandinsky, used intense colors to depict an interior, abstract universe—inspired by his native island of Hydra—in a similar way that Kandinsky and Paul Klee depicted the abstract grace of Tunisia. Ghika was a character in Henry Miller's *The Colossus of Maroussi*. I remembered that Fermor had dedicated *Between the Woods and the Water* to him.

We went outside to the sprawling terrace, where pebbles and stones had been laid out in delightful geometries to form recesses and panoramic spots for luncheons and summer dinner parties. I thought of the conversations that had occurred here among Fermor, Durrell, Stark, Ghika, the Nobel Prize–winning poet George Seferis, and other literary and intellectual grandees. Behind us, Taygetus rose steeply in dark shadows as the sea on three sides slapped against the rocks below. There was a table of blue and white Iberian tiles set against the house, an invitation to sit down and read or have a drink.

"It was after the war, the Greek Civil War, I mean," he said, following my gaze across the terrace. "Joan and I had come over the Taygetus from Sparta."

"By car?" I cut in naively.

"God, no. We were on foot, walking, for days. We had descended from the mountains and found this spot. Later we met these wonderful workmen. One of them was my *koumbaros* [best man] at my wedding. Property was really cheap back then. I designed the terrace myself. The olive groves here are very, very old. We had to uproot a number of trees to build the house. When we replanted them, all but one took root."

He led me back into the house, up and down small staircases, in and out of other rooms with their own, smaller terraces. His vigorous steps made the years evaporate. It was suddenly easy to imagine him covering the entire span of Europe on foot. I saw other, veritable caverns of battered old editions: the complete works of Henry James, Rudyard Kipling, and T. S. Eliot, scores upon scores of guidebooks among obscure volumes on Near Eastern history, Indian art, and so forth. Noticing volumes of *The Hungarian Quarterly* piled in one room to eye level, I asked if he had read them.

"Heavens, no. The books just arrive. I can't get rid of them. I've lost the ability to keep them in any order. It takes me an hour to find anything now. It's so discouraging. But I won't discard them." Of course not. They all reminded him of someplace he had been. I remember meeting an old World War II correspondent, the floor of whose living room in Cape Ann had been covered in newspaper clippings, in the hopeless task of keeping abreast of events in every country he had reported from: nearly half the world.

"Here is where the real work gets done."

We were now in a whitewashed room, adjacent to the main terrace. It was crawling with books and crowded with tables supporting stacks of papers, including part of a manuscript. An Olivetti typewriter in fine working condition was the only concession to twentieth-century office technology.

"It was New Year's Day, 1935, when I arrived in Constantinople, just before my twentieth birthday. . . ." He had started drifting. His coals had begun to dim, I realized. I should have caught him some years earlier. Yet he was still sharp where it counted: criticizing a recent travel book on Eastern Europe that lay nearby because it had failed to note some poet from Bucovina of whom I had never heard. Nevertheless, I worried that his much-awaited final volume, which he had been working on for so long, might never be completed. When I asked—noticing the wildflowers through the window—about the name of a plant I had seen long ago at Mistra and could not identify, he tore at his memory for a few moments, declaring finally, cheerfully: "I have become a martyr to scatter-brained oblivion."

We wandered to another room, where he showed me some original drawings by the nineteenth-century English humorist and artist Edward Lear, famous for his sketches of the Levant: another gift, I was told. This whole magnificent house, so much more impressive than those of wealthier people I have met over the years, was less a consequence of financial means than of the intrepid brilliance of Patrick and his wife, Joan, who was ill the day of my visit. I thought of Durrell's description in *Bitter Lemons* of the "magpies" on Cyprus: not birds but fellow expatriates who had ransacked the Mediterranean and the Near East, bringing back "a bewildering medley of objects, from Egyptian *musarabiyas* to Turkish mosque-lamps," in order to decorate their salons and studies as part of the "formidable task" of making the "'perfect house for a writer to live in.'" Fermor's house was a monument not to status, but to a sanctified existence.

"I hope I've given you ideas for further reading," he said, leading me out to my car.

"And you?"

"I'm reading a lot of verse these days." His expression was full of sublime memories. I had more to ask him, but he looked tired and I remembered his mention of a siesta. "The afternoon is the time for real sleep," he had written in *Mani*.

☙❧

The weather had changed by the time I left Kardamyli. The wind now crushed against the trees and the overcast sky made me want to duck my head as it met the granite-colored water. I drove northward for an hour in a downpour until Kalamata. It was another ninety minutes westward through rolling olive groves until, descending a mountain in a series of switchbacks, the crater-like Bay of Navarino appeared like a lick of gold as the clouds broke near sunset and color poured back into the landscape. Pylos, at the edge of the bay, was a cluster of white houses in the sheeted mist. There I found a hotel with creaking floor boards and a view of the bay that reminded me of John Masefield's poem "Sea Fever." I stayed up late working on a draft of the day's notes while my recollections were still vivid.

Fermor had found his way, and his way could not be replicated. But there are riches enough for all of us, no matter our abilities and circumstances. It is only the inspiration that requires summoning.

# RECOMMENDED READING

Ammianus, Marcellinus. *History: Books 20–26.* Translated by
John C. Rolfe. Harvard University Press, Cambridge,
Massachusetts, 1940.

Andrews, Kevin. *The Flight of Ikaros: Travels in Greece During a
Civil War.* Houghton Mifflin, Boston, 1959.

Auden, W. H. *The Double Man.* Random House, New York,
1941.

Augustine, Saint. *The City of God.* Translated by Marcus Dobs.
Modern Library, New York, 1994.

———. *The Confessions.* Translated by John K. Ryan. Image/
Doubleday, New York, 1960.

Barzun, Jacques. *From Dawn to Decadence: 500 Years of Western
Cultural Life; 1500 to the Present.* HarperCollins, New York,
2000.

Bergson, Henri. *Matter and Memory.* Translated by N. M. Paul and
    W. S. Palmer. Zone Books, New York, (1908) 1991.

Bowra, C. Maurice. *The Greek Experience.* The World Publishing
    Company, New York, 1957.

Bradford, Ernle. *Mediterranean: Portrait of a Sea.* Harcourt, New
    York, 1971.

Braudel, Fernand. *The Mediterranean and the Mediterranean World
    in the Age of Philip II.* Volume I. Translated by Sian Reynolds.
    Harper & Row, New York, (1949) 1972.

Byron, Robert. *The Station: Athos; Treasures and Men.* With an
    Introduction by Christopher Sykes. Knopf, New York,
    (1928) 1949.

Byron, Robert, and David Talbot Rice. *The Birth of Western
    Painting: A History of Colour, Form, and Iconography, Illustrated
    from the Paintings of Mistra and Mount Athos, of Giotto and
    Duccio, and of El Greco.* Knopf, New York, 1931.

Cavarnos, Constantine. *Orthodox Iconography.* Institute for Byzantine
    and Modern Greek Studies, Belmont, Massachusetts, 1977.

Chatzidakis, Manolis. *Mystras: The Medieval City and the Castle.*
    Ekdotike Athenon, Athens, 1981.

Clark, Eleanor. *Rome and a Villa.* Atheneum, New York, 1950.

Clogg, Richard. *A Short History of Modern Greece.* Cambridge
    University Press, New York, 1979.

Cronin, Vincent. *The Golden Honeycomb.* E. P. Dutton, New York,
    1954.

Davenport, Fionn. *Sicily.* Lonely Planet, Oakland, California, 2000.

Douglas, Norman. *Siren Land and Fountains in the Sand.* Secker
    and Warburg, London, (1911 and 1912) 1957.

Dumas, Alexandre. *The Count of Monte Cristo,* 1846.

Durrell, Lawrence. *Bitter Lemons.* Faber and Faber, London, 1957.

————. *Sicilian Carousel.* Faber and Faber, London, 1977.

————. *Spirit of Place: Letters and Essays on Travel.* Edited by Alan
    G. Thomas. E. P. Dutton, New York, 1971.

Faerna, Jose Maria. *Klee.* Cameo/Abrams, New York, 1996.

Fanon, Frantz. *The Wretched of the Earth.* Grove Press, New York, 1963.

Fantar, Mhamed Hassine. *Tunisia: Crossroads of Civilizations.* National Archaeological and Art Institute, Tunis, 1992.

Fermor, Patrick Leigh. *Between the Woods and the Water: On Foot to Constantinople; From the Middle Danube to the Iron Gates.* John Murray, London, 1986.

————. *Mani: Travels in the Southern Peloponnese.* John Murray, London, 1958.

————. *Roumeli: Travels in Northern Greece.* John Murray, London, 1966.

————. *A Time of Gifts: On Foot to Constantinople; From the Hook of Holland to the Middle Danube.* John Murray, London, 1977.

Flaubert, Gustave. *Salammbô.* Translated by A. J. Krailsheimer. Penguin Books, New York, (1862) 1977. Some of the quotations I used come from a 1931 translation by J. C. Chartres, published by E. P. Dutton, New York.

Fox, Robert. *The Inner Sea: The Mediterranean and Its People.* Knopf, New York, 1993.

Frazer, James George. *The Golden Bough: A Study in Magic and Religion.* Macmillan, London, 1922.

Fussell, Paul. *Abroad: British Literary Traveling Between the Wars.* Oxford University Press, New York, 1980.

Gage, Nicholas. *Hellas: A Portrait of Greece.* Efstathiadis Group, Athens, 1987.

Geertz, Clifford. *Islam Observed.* University of Chicago Press, Chicago, (1968) 1971.

Geniesse, Jane Fletcher. *Passionate Nomad: The Life of Freya Stark.* Random House, New York, 1999.

Gibbon, Edward. *The Decline and Fall of the Roman Empire.* Volumes 1–3. Everyman/Knopf, New York, 1910.

Gide, André. *Amyntas: North African Journals.* Translated by
    Richard Howard. The Ecco Press, New York, (1906) 1988.
————. *The Immoralist.* Translated by Richard Howard. Knopf,
    New York, (1921) 1970.
Goethe, Johann Wolfgang von. *Italian Journey: 1786–1788.*
    Translated by W. H. Auden and Elizabeth Mayer. William
    Collins Sons, London, 1962.
Graves, Robert. *The Greek Myths: 1 & 2.* Penguin Books, New
    York, 1955.
————. *The White Goddess: A Historical Grammar of Poetic Myth.*
    Farrar, Straus and Giroux, New York, (1948) 1966.
Gress, David. *From Plato to NATO: The Idea of the West and Its
    Opponents.* The Free Press, New York, 1998.
Guido, Margaret. *Sicily: An Archaeological Guide: The Prehistoric
    and Roman Remains and the Greek Cities.* Faber and Faber,
    London, 1967.
Hamilton, Edith. *The Greek Way.* Norton, New York, 1930.
Hanson, Victor Davis. *Carnage and Culture: Landmark Battles in
    the Rise of Western Power.* Doubleday, New York, 2001.
Homer. *The Iliad.* Translated by Robert Fagles. Viking, New
    York, 1990.
————. *The Odyssey.* Translated by Robert Fagles. Viking, New
    York, 1996.
Ibn Khaldun. *The Muqaddimah: An Introduction to History.*
    Translated by Franz Rosenthal. With an Introduction by
    N. J. Dawood. Bollingen/Princeton University Press,
    Princeton, New Jersey, (1958) 1967.
Kagan, Donald. *The Peace of Nicias and the Sicilian Expedition.*
    Cornell University Press, Ithaca, New York, 1981.
Kazantzakis, Nikos. *Journeying: Travels in Italy, Egypt,
    Sinai, Jerusalem and Cyprus.* Translated by Themi Vasils
    and Theodora Vasils. Little, Brown, Boston, (1961)
    1975.

Klee, Paul. *The Diaries of Paul Klee: 1898–1918.* University of California Press, Berkeley, California, 1964.

Lampedusa, Giuseppe di. *The Leopard.* Translated by Archibald Colquhoun. Pantheon, New York, 1960.

Le Normand-Romain, Antoinette. *Rodin: At the Musée Rodin.* Éditions Scala, Paris, 1996.

Livy. *The War with Hannibal.* Translated by Aubrey de Selincourt. Penguin, New York, 1965.

Lucas, F. L. *Greek Tragedy and Comedy.* Viking, New York, (1954) 1967.

MacDonald, William L., and John A. Pinto. *Hadrian's Villa and Its Legacy.* Yale University Press, New Haven, Connecticut, 1995.

Martin, John Rupert. *Baroque.* Westview Press, Boulder, Colorado, 1977.

Miller, Henry. *The Colossus of Maroussi.* Secker & Warburg, London, 1942.

Missac, Pierre. *Walter Benjamin's Passages.* Translated by Shierry Weber Nicholsen. MIT Press, Cambridge, Massachusetts, (1987) 1995.

Montesquieu. *The Spirit of the Laws.* Translated by Anne M. Cohler, Basia Carolyn Miller, and Harold Samuel Stone. Cambridge University Press, New York, (1748) 1989.

Moss, W. Stanley. *Ill Met by Moonlight.* Harrap & Company, London, 1950.

Norwich, John Julius. *A History of Venice.* Knopf, New York, 1977 and 1981.

———. *The Kingdom in the Sun: 1130–1194.* Harper & Row, New York, 1970.

———. *The Other Conquest.* Harper & Row, New York, 1967.

Oliver, Jeanne. *Croatia.* Lonely Planet, Oakland, California, 1999.

Petrarch. *Selections from the Canzoniere and Other Works.* Translated and with an Introduction by Mark Musa. Oxford University Press, New York, 1985.

Plutarch. *The Lives of the Noble Grecians and Romans.* Volume II. Translated by John Dryden. Modern Library, New York, (1683–86) 1992.

Pound, Ezra. *Selected Cantos.* New Directions, New York, 1966.

Praga, Giuseppe. *History of Dalmatia.* Giardini, Pisa, Italy, (1954) 1993.

Proust, Marcel. *Swann's Way.* Translated by C. K. Scott Moncrieff. Modern Library, New York, 1928.

Puglisi, Catherine. *Caravaggio.* Phaidon Press, London, 1998.

Raven, Susan. *Rome in Africa.* Evans Brothers, London, 1969.

Rilke, Rainer Maria. *Lettres à Rodin.* Préface de Georges Grappe. Editions Émile-Paul Frères/Bartavelle, Paris, 1930.

———. *Rodin.* Grey Walls Press, London, 1946.

Robb, Peter. *Midnight in Sicily.* Duffy & Snellgrove, New South Wales, Australia, 1996.

Runciman, Steven. *Mistra: Byzantine Capital of the Peloponnese.* Thames and Hudson, London, 1980.

———. *The Sicilian Vespers: A History of the Mediterranean World in the Later Thirteenth Century.* Cambridge University Press, Cambridge, England, 1958.

Senior, Michael. *Greece and Its Myths.* Victor Gollancz, London, 1978.

Sherrard, Philip. *The Greek East and the Latin West: A Study in the Christian Tradition.* Oxford University Press, London, 1959.

Simeti, Mary Taylor. *On Persephone's Island: A Sicilian Journal.* Knopf, New York, 1986.

Stendhal. *Memoirs of a Tourist.* Translated by Allan Seager. Northwestern University Press, Chicago, (1838) 1962.

Stevens, Wallace. *The Collected Poems.* Knopf, New York, 1954.

———. *Harmonium.* Knopf, New York, 1923.

Strassler, Robert B. *The Landmark Thucydides: A Comprehensive Guide to the Peloponnesian War.* Translated by Richard Crawley. The Free Press, New York, (1874) 1996.

Tennyson, Alfred, Lord. *The Works of Alfred, Lord Tennyson.* Macmillan, London, 1892.

Theroux, Paul. *The Pillars of Hercules: A Grand Tour of the Mediterranean.* Ballantine, New York, 1995.

Thucydides. *The Peloponnesian War.* Translated by Thomas Hobbes. University of Michigan Press, Ann Arbor, Michigan, (1629) 1959.

Travirka, Antun. *Split: History, Culture, Art Heritage.* Forum, Zadar, Croatia, 2000.

Virgil. *The Aeneid.* Translated by Robert Fitzgerald. Random House, New York, 1981.

Ware, Timothy. *The Orthodox Church.* Penguin Books, New York, 1963.

West, Rebecca. *Black Lamb and Grey Falcon.* Viking, New York, 1941.

Willett, David. *Tunisia.* Lonely Planet, Oakland, California, 1998.

Wills, Garry. *Saint Augustine.* Viking, New York, 1999.

Woodhouse, C. M. *George Gemistos Plethon: The Last of the Hellenes.* Oxford University Press, New York, 1986.

Yourcenar, Marguerite. *Memoirs of Hadrian.* Translated by Grace Frick. Farrar, Straus and Giroux, New York, (1951) 1963.

Zeraffa, Michel. *Tunisia.* Translated by R. A. Deam. Viking, New York, 1965.

# INDEX